Once upon a
Chicken Pie

AND OTHER FOOD TALES

This book is dedicated to all the food lovers and travellers around the world who have either knowingly or unwittingly inspired us.

JOHAN DE VILLIERS WITH LEN STRAW

Published in 2010 by Struik Lifestyle
(an imprint of Random House Struik (Pty) Ltd)
Company Reg. No. 1966/003153/07
80 McKenzie Street, Cape Town, 8001
PO Box 1144, Cape Town, 8000, South Africa

PUBLISHER: Linda de Villiers
EDITOR: Cecilia Barfield
DESIGNER: Beverley Dodd
PHOTOGRAPHER: Ryno
PROOFREADER AND INDEXER: Joy Clack

Reproduction: Hirt & Carter Cape (Pty) Ltd
Printing and binding: Tien Wah Press (Pte) Ltd, Singapore

ISBN 978-1-77007-850-5

www.randomstruik.co.za

Contents

OREWORD

It was in the old Huguenot town of Franschhoek, in a tiny, elegant hotel that we met two uniquely gifted characters who were the heart and soul of the establishment. They managed everything to perfection. Their daily focus centred on the comfort and well-being of their guests as though it were their own home.

Len with his infectious, effervescent nature was there to greet us and place us under their protection, while Johan with his gentle, smiling eyes – Jasper, his beloved greyhound at his side – welcomed us with all his heart. If a shadow of concern flickered across his brow, it was merely to be assured that everything was to our liking.

I was so entranced by the beauty that enveloped me, I recall traipsing behind Johan like a puppy into his kitchen, his domain. And it was there, with the light streaming through the open windows, the heady aroma of the sun-ripened fruits and freshly harvested herbs piled in abundance on great platters like a Dutch still life, that I had found Nirvarna. This kitchen was a hive of happy industry where Johan encouraged apprentices while he stirred the pots, tasted sauces and conjured up his dishes.

Try to imagine the pleasure of my first morning. Peacefully refreshed after our long flight, we came down to a breakfast table that Matisse should have painted: bunches of wild flowers gathered that morning and popped into a vase, an assortment of the prettiest flowered china rescued from bric-a-brac shops by the incomparable eye of Johan and Len during their years of browsing. They were living the Buddhist teaching: 'To truly give from one's heart, one must not merely offer, but must bestow a gift, unbidden at the feet of the guest.'

In this book you will find far more than a compendium of recipes. It is a collection of a lifetime, appreciating the skill of cooking, understanding the alchemy that ties food together; that the right twist of lime, a thread of saffron and few torn leaves of tarragon can make a dish sing. Inspiration came to Johan at the knee of his mother, and from his sister Voy's passion for cooking delicious, Afrikaans food for the family. Throughout his years of travel, his repertoire broadened and expanded, finally realising that truthful food is the best and that good cooking, in the end, is an act of love.

PATSY PUTTNAM

NTRODUCTION

Lennie and I have been blessed with creative spirits, minds and hands. Thirsty for inspiration and information, we love travelling. In bothersome, impecuniary times, we rely on books and magazines to keep us buoyant. Our families and friends are also invaluable in this respect and not a day passes without us being touched by a kindred spirit. Our French-style tea and coffee shop, la Petite Tarte, miraculously attracts guests who we not only relate to, but also grow fond of, or in the case of foreign visitors, we are very sad to bid adieu.

Our lives have been filled with opportunities. Len worked as a bookkeeper, in retailing at Harrods, created beautiful displays at the old Stuttafords, moved into PR and managed a shopping centre. He established a charming deli/take-away called Straws, which grew into a fully fledged restaurant in Cavendish Square. But eventually the creative urge triumphed and he started his career in painting, both pictures and interiors.

When I left Stellenbosch University in 1969, I worked as a designer at a firm of architects – but only until I had enough money for my *grande tour* of Europe. Ten months and ten million unforgettable experiences later, I returned to Cape Town. Four days after my return I took up a position as lecturer in jewellery-making at the Ruth Prowse Art Centre run by the jovial, capable and well-loved Erik Laubscher, who nurtured a unique environment of creativity. I also grabbed the opportunity of working in the costume props department of the Cape Performing Arts Board. More interaction with talented designers and artists!

Some 18 years of teaching at government schools followed, working with children through to young adults, and always trusting that they enjoyed themselves as much as I did. In the meantime, Len's decorative painting studio grew and grew and the temptation to join him was overwhelming.

Together we established a successful studio-base from where we taught, executed commissions and compiled three books. A successful sideline of Len's was ChinaWorks, where he and Belinda Wilkinson produced hand-painted china. The harder we worked, the more frequently we could visit friends in Greece and Egypt. Painting contracts followed in Cyprus, Paris, New York and finally on Skiathos, which saw us helping to establish Villa Athena. That was followed by two years of running the villa and its self-catering cottages. It was hard work, but we met wonderful people and cemented everlasting friendships.

On our return to South Africa, we joined the Royal Portfolio as managers of La Residence in Franschhoek. Once more we were blessed with beautiful surroundings, gentle guests and magnificent experiences. After seven years we moved back to our Cape Town home. Cristiana, daughter of our friend Lina, was ready to sell her lovely *salon du thé* and coffee shop to us and we jumped at the opportunity to be independent again. la Petite Tarte seems to attract a most pleasant, refined clientele, we see our friends regularly and treasured old friends have been coming back into our lives.

A delightful aspect of growing older is the facility to look back. I presume that it is a universal phenomenon to discard, or pass on, more and more chattels, treasure or junk – whatever clutters one's 'later' world. This world of mine produced little notebooks, slips of paper, itineraries, museum tickets, photographs and many memories of our very own history. Precious as these are to us, Len and I worked together to record them and present them to others who may enjoy them with us.

The recipes all have connotations of feasts, family meals, gatherings of friends or quiet tables *à deux*. Some dishes have always been around, others are new and some have reappeared. Therein lies the fascinating quality of food. To have others at one's table and to entertain them with food, drink and hospitality is a privilege and a gift. Passing on a few of 'our' recipes is an extension of that. The title,'Once Upon a Chicken Pie', Lennie says, 'fell out of the sky', a thought that came to him. It had immediate appeal though and inspired the link to the children's rhymes and story titles. Once the child in us was awoken, it was unstoppable!

Never at a loss for a dream or two, we will forever want to go back to visit our friends overseas, to discover new places, to enjoy our home, to do things to it, and to paint, cook, listen to music, string up some beads, scratch in the garden and spoil some doggies again.

At least one little dream has come to fruition: this book!

JOHAN DE VILLIERS

Once Upon a Chicken Pie

An oil painting we bought in Cairo (left), and our first view of Skiathos harbour from the ferry (below).

CHICKEN PIE AFTER MIDNIGHT

Early in the summer season of 2001 – the new Villa Athena not yet on the tourist map – we were quiet. Skiathos was becoming busier by the day, and shopkeepers stretched their days longer and longer … making the most of trade-on-tap. Takis and Niki, our dear friends from the city of Volos, had opened a third shop that year and were weary even before the season began.

We wanted to reward them for their kindness and invited them to dine with us. Our time was flexible, theirs was ruled by the shops. Lennie asked Takis when they would like to join us for a meal. After various protracted consultations with Niki, Giorgos, Theologia and Poppie (real name Caliope, after one of the nine Muses) – all involved in the running of the shops – an appropriate time was chosen.

'We come for lunch at 12 o'clock!'

'Oh,' said Lennie, 'a midday meal then?'

'No, no,' said Takis, 'the night lunch …!'

And so they arrived at Villa Athena at 12.00, 12.30 and 1.00 in the dead of night. With them came two friends who play in the State Symphony Orchestra of Thessaloniki. Oh goodness, we thought, two eccentric Greek musicians. To our surprise, however, both were young, attractive and pleasant, only one of them being slightly eccentric and the other a little melancholy. This was the start of a most significant friendship with Yannis and Mimis.

Skiathos harbour

The main ingredient of a successful dinner party fell into our laps! Jovial and handsome Takis, Niki with her beautiful lilting operatic voice, bird-like and petite Theologia twittering in Gringlish, Giorgos's low, serious voice as percussion, Poppie with her drama-training doing the hot-potato, Mimis sounding like his violin rapidly speaking in Greek, English and French, while Yannis in true cello-style provided a steady sensible tone to it all. And that all before the wine …

We were concerned that our friends might not enjoy outlandish food. On the other hand, I did not feel myself capable of producing a genuine Greek meal. Eventually we offered them a salad of ripe tomatoes and fresh basil from our kitchen garden, slices of fried Melinzana with thick yoghurt and origanum (freshly picked in the mountains that afternoon), and something that I introduced as 'kotopita' – chicken pie. I had made the word up, but they assured me that that was exactly what it was. Instead of making a large pie using layers and layers of phyllo pastry, I created individual parcels of filling wrapped in buttery phyllo with a honey-brown twist to crown each one. This was old hat back home in Cape Town, but our Greek friends loved it! The filling was flavoured with tarragon – a herb not too frequently used in Greek cuisine – and enriched with some sour cream.

Our wonderful friend, Takis.

'The same,' the guests concluded, 'but not the same. *Poli oreia* (very good), Jo-han!'

Sadly, we had no left-overs for the real 12 o'clock lunch the next day.

$\mathcal{T}$ARRAGON CHICKEN PIE
in phyllo

30 ml sunflower oil
1 large chicken
2 sticks celery, cut into 4-cm pieces
3 medium carrots, cleaned and sliced
2 leeks, topped, tailed and thinly sliced
10 ml dried tarragon
1 litre water
salt
45 ml cake flour
500 g phyllo pastry
125 g butter, melted

Pour the oil into a saucepan and heat on medium heat. Brown the chicken in the saucepan, turning from time to time to sear all over.

Add the vegetables and tarragon, then pour the water over the chicken. Add a little salt. Simmer until the chicken is really tender, falling off the bone. Remove the chicken and leave to cool down. Strain the liquid, discarding the vegetables. Leave to stand until all the fat has risen to the top, then skim it off.

Return the saucepan to the stove with the strained liquid and boil until this 'stock' has reduced to ±750 ml, then top up with 250 ml water to make 1 litre of liquid.

Bone and skin the chicken, reserving all the good, solid meat and set it aside. Preheat the oven to 180 °C.

Whisk the flour into the reduced stock and bring it to the boil, stirring constantly to avoid lumps from forming. Pour this thickened sauce over the chicken and mix well. Leave to cool. Place 12 sheets of the phyllo pastry on a cutting board and cut them in half. Brush a sheet with a little melted butter, then place another sheet on top of it at an angle and brush with butter. Repeat twice more, i.e. you should have a 'staggered stack' of 4 sheets. Scoop about 3 tablespoons (45 ml) of the chicken filling into the centre. Gather the outer edges of the pastry together and close them over the filling to form a pouch, twisting the pastry to close it. Make 5 more of these pouches.

Arrange the pouches on a baking tray and brush any leftover melted butter over them. Bake for about 15 minutes, but do take care as phyllo pastry can darken very suddenly. The parcels should be pale golden in colour. Serve with roasted vine tomatoes and wilted spinach leaves. Serves 6 as a main course

PHILIP'S CHICKEN PIE

1 whole chicken (±1.5 kg), cut into portions
salt and pepper to taste
30 ml butter
1 onion, chopped
8 peppercorns
3 blades mace or 5 ml ground mace
6 allspice berries
500 ml water
125 ml dry white wine
1 egg, beaten
juice of 1 lemon
2 hard-boiled eggs, roughly chopped
4 slices gypsy ham, chopped

TOPPING
1 egg, beaten
125 ml oil
125 ml milk
120 g cake flour
10 ml baking powder
3 ml mustard powder
salt

Season the chicken portions with the salt and pepper. Fry each portion in the butter in a heavy saucepan, to seal. Remove the chicken from the saucepan.

Brown the onion in the same saucepan, then return the chicken pieces together with the peppercorns, mace and allspice. Pour in the water and wine. Bring to the boil, then cover and simmer until the chicken is very tender. Turn the heat off, remove the chicken from the saucepan and leave to cool. Skin and debone the chicken, and flake the flesh.

Whisk the beaten egg with the lemon juice, then add a little (about 125 ml) of the warm cooking liquid. Stir the egg mixture into the liquid in the saucepan. Cook, stirring over a low heat until slightly thickened. Add the flaked chicken to the sauce. Pour the mixture into an ovenproof baking dish and sprinkle with the chopped eggs and ham.

Preheat the oven to 180 °C.

For the topping, whisk together the egg (reserve a little for brushing), oil and milk. Sift the dry ingredients together, then add to the egg mixture. Mix thoroughly, but do not overwork. Cover the chicken with spoonfuls of the batter (they should look like scones).

Brush lightly with the left-over beaten egg and bake for 30 minutes. Serve with yellow rice and seasonal vegetables. Serves 6 as a main course

Our late friend Philip du Toit in contemplative mood on my balcony in Mouille Point, Cape Town, 1969.

The Monastery of Evangelistria in the mountains above Skiathos,
and (opposite) a ceramic sculpture by John Knowers.

ΕΛΛΗΝΙΚΟΝ

Από το 1938

Yannis and the Beanstalk

Churches on Mykonos (top), and traditional open-work, cotton curtains at Villa Ella, Skiathos (bottom).

We did not at first realise that there is a distinct difference between the overwhelming hospitality and generosity of Greek people, and genuine long-term friendships. All newcomers are entitled to the first. *Xenia* (hospitality) is a given; only a Greek with shoddy manners will deny a stranger that. Real friendship, however, needs to be earned. The process involves many nights of ouzo and *mezethes* (tasty morsels), talking and talking into the wee hours, disagreements, little gifts, solicited and unsolicited advice, kind gestures and a few put-downs – in fact, all the aspects that enhance and test a friendship. And that takes time, but it lasts.

Such was the friendship we built up with Yannis (not the same Yannis as referred to on p. 7), Maria and their daughters. There is no doubt that our love affair with Skiathos would have been lacking were it not for them.

They are pillars of the community, hoteliers, entrepreneurs, villagers, but above all, hardworking farmers. They have sheep, goats, orchards, vegetable and flower gardens, vines, chickens, geese and even kept turkeys until Maria decided they should be no more! Petite Maria cooks and bakes, she knits, crochets and enjoys home crafts. She nurses lambs, collects eggs, harvests olives and fruits, launders and cleans. Happiness, for her, is being busy.

Yannis is the same. His big, strong hands can drive an earth digger or nurture a chick. He does not do things in half-measures and, as he ages, it probably shows. But he remains a handsome man; the blonde hair is greying, but the blue eyes still sparkle. As he reminisces about his youth on the island, one conjures up visions of the Golden Greek: blonde, blue-eyed, fishing, swimming and charming the young girls! The Cat from Skiathos! His wise sayings all find their context in farm life. For instance, a boy was once described as too stupid to divide the hay between two horses, or explaining the awkward situation he and Maria were in when they each had to stay in a hotel they had to run, separated and missing each other, he maintained, 'Oh well, one cannot keep the bull with the cows all the time!'

Since I grew up with a dearest father who was a farmer at heart, I have a lot of love, respect and admiration for farmers. Yannis understood this and loved talking about his farm, the animals and fruit trees. He showed me the trenches, the new, budding vines, the rich, crumbly compost and the new patch of broad beans. The bushes were lush and bearing with such fecundity that he could not harvest them quickly enough. Yannis threw a plastic bag at me and commanded, 'Pick!' I did. At half-a-bag full I hesitated – one should not be too grabby. 'Pick! he said again. And I did. Until the bag overflowed.

Then we had an *ouzaki* (a local drink) while I was shown how to prepare Yannis's beans. 'It's not good,' he explained, 'if you do not take many …,' which I discovered was dill. Such was our introduction to the many bean dishes of the traditional Greek kitchen.

WHITE BEAN PÂTÉ

500 g fresh shelled white beans
1 large leek or 3 shallots
2 fresh or 4 dried bay leaves
125 ml virgin olive oil

4 spring onions, finely chopped
50 g flat-leaf parsley, finely chopped
2 sprigs of thyme, finely chopped
salt and pepper to taste

Boil the beans, leek (or shallots) and bay leaves in plenty of water until the beans are very soft. Skim off any impurities from time to time. The beans will need at least 40 minutes to soften. Drain the beans, reserving a small quantity of the cooking liquid, but discard the leek (or shallots) and bay leaves.

Place the beans and about half of the oil into a food processor, and blend into a smooth mixture. (Use a little of the cooking liquid to achieve a light, almost frothy, mixture.) Add the spring onions and herbs, and blend. Season to taste.

Decant the mixture into a shallow dish and drizzle the rest of the oil over the entire surface. This prevents it from drying out and becoming seriously unattractive. Garnish as you wish.

Enjoy the pâté with warm pita bread, lashings of olive oil, a squeeze of lemon juice, more chopped spring onions, herbs, a jug of village wine … and some villagers! Serves 6 as a starter

YANNIS'S BROAD BEANS

500 g very young, fresh whole broad beans or fresh shelled broad beans
125 ml virgin olive oil
1 large onion, peeled and sliced
2 large potatoes, peeled and cubed
2 large (Yannis-sized!) handfuls fresh dill, roughly chopped
a little grated nutmeg
salt to taste
ground white pepper to taste

The beans I got from Yannis were young and tender. All I needed to do was to top and tail them, and discard the string along the seam of those pods that did not quite pass the infantile test. Should your fresh shelled beans be slightly past their prime, dunk them in boiling water to loosen their skins. Remove the skins with their 'eyes'. This is a seemingly thankless task, but one with great returns! Cut the beans into 4-cm lengths.

Heat the olive oil in a saucepan and braise the onion slices over a medium heat until golden and almost melting. Add the potatoes and braise for a few minutes.

Stir in the beans until covered in oil, then braise. Keep a moderate heat going, adding a small amount of water in order to stew the dish. Do not cover the saucepan, but stir occasionally and simmer gently. If necessary, add more drops of water from time to time to keep a little sauce bubbling.

Once the vegetables are really tender, you could squash a few pieces of potato to thicken the sauce. Add the dill, nutmeg, salt and pepper. (Be warned, use white pepper modestly. A small quantity will impart all the lovely fragrant, spicy taste that's required.)

As soon as the dill is thoroughly wilted and mixed in, transfer the beans to a serving dish. Yannis was so generous with his gift and advice that we could hardly wait for this minute and enjoyed our dish while it was hot.

The next day at lunch we had (much) more of the same at room temperature with crusty bread and feta cheese. The flavours had melded and improved greatly overnight. A drizzle of olive oil and a squeeze of lemon later, there were no more beans left to spill … only full tummies, happy memories and oily chins!

Over time I have made this recipe mine by varying it on occasion. Sometimes I use leeks instead of onions, or I add 2 tablespoons (30 ml) of ouzo along with the dill. At other times I combine whole baby artichokes or trimmed fresh artichokes

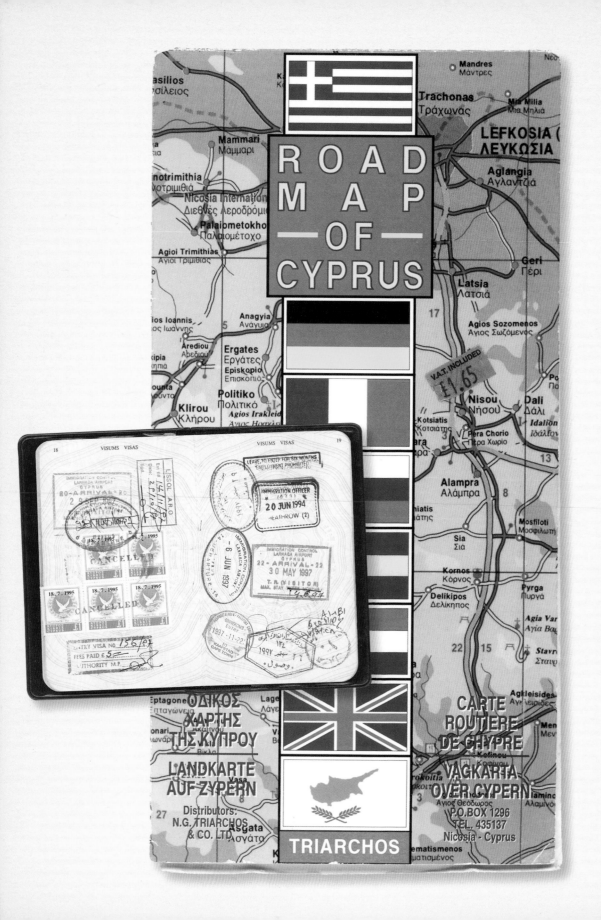

Youthful Capers

In 1986 we published a book on decorative paint effects. As it was specifically aimed at the South African market, and was a collaboration between ourselves and a local paint manufacturer, we were sponsored to travel throughout the country to promote both the book as well as various new products developed by the paint firm. Delightful (and delighted!) people from all over the country attended these courses in which we all had great fun producing our own sample boards, rolling, ragging, gilding and sponging.

A young woman from one of the Johannesburg classes enquired whether we would consider running these courses 'overseas'. 'Oh yes,' we responded, but where did she have in mind?

'Cyprus,' she said.

'Cyprus?' we pondered.

Our annual trip to Greece was already in the planning, with three of our sisters. The aim was to show them two of our favourite destinations – Egypt and Greece. None of us will ever forget the joys of that jaunt! On the way home, we left the sisters in Cairo while we flew to Larnaca in Cyprus. There Irene welcomed us with laughter, kindness and overwhelming generosity. It never ceases to amaze me how at home we felt in Cyprus – leading me to consider the possibility of a previous life in the Levant. Over time we paid another two visits to Cyprus, on each occasion discovering more about this enchanting island. That is how we came to know about capers.

On our walks we encountered a type of bush that thrives on rock faces in which the roots penetrate cracks, nooks and crannies. For such a barren location these plants are surprisingly lush and the flowers are nothing short of spectacular. Sometimes they trail and cascade over the rocks, frequently quite inaccessible. The leaves are grey-green in colour, slightly waxy and apparently delicate. In the spring sculptural buds appear, opening into the most delicate pink bird-of-paradise flowers. As they fade, the berries form. The downside of the caper bush lies in its thorns. Snaking your hands into the bush to harvest the buds, berries or sprigs is quite easy. Getting them out again is not! The thorns point inwards, catching at your hands as you withdraw.

The rugged beauty of homes on Cyprus.

Pickled or salted capers, as we know them, refer to the buds. Less well known are the berries on their elegantly curved stalks. They need to be harvested once fully formed, but not overblown and 'dry'. The tender sprigs may also be used; the last three pairs of leaves on new sprouts are harvested and pickled. Although these are thorny, pickling softens the thorns, which are perfectly edible, if somewhat rough on the tongue.

Once we got to know the caper bushes of Cyprus, we developed an awareness that enabled us to spot them on the islands of Skiathos and Alonissos, along the coast of Puglia, as well as various other locations where the conditions support them.

A delightful caper story that amused us no end was that of Carol, a dear friend who travelled to Italy to escape the boredom of the hairdressing world in Cape Town. Italy was the chosen destination, not only for its culture, fashion and food, but most probably also for its handsome men! On their own in Milan, Carol and her friend Jessica were delighted to be invited to dinner by a kind gentleman friend of a mutual acquaintance in Cape Town. They dressed up beautifully, looked stunning and enjoyed a lovely evening. Quite taken with the two pretty young women, their vivacity and joyfulness, he suggested that they take a trip to the island of Pantelleria where they could enjoy a holiday in his holiday home. They hesitated; there was the small matter of insufficient funds, and they did not even know how to get there! He assured them they would have two flight tickets by the next morning and that he would very much like to sponsor their Pantelleria excursion. The following morning two tickets awaited them at reception, transfers were in place and paid for, as was their accommodation for the past few nights.

Pantelleria, the southernmost Italian island and barren in a Mediterranean way, produces the finest capers. It was most welcoming to our friends. Carol and Jessica got to know the locals, enjoyed lengthy lunches, late dinners and danced on the café tables … It's little wonder that Carol gained a reputation on the island as the ballerina!

As in all good fairy tales, the ballerina found a beau and together they picked some of the best capers in the world for the rest of their lives. Youthful capers!

———— ∞∞∞ ————

I tend to enjoy capers as little accents in salads and sweet tomato dishes, as a counterfoil for the earthy blandness of potatoes, and as accompaniments to egg and fish dishes. The tiniest capers, usually pickled, are called 'nonpareilles' and they truly are just that. Salted, capers can last for ages, but they must be rinsed well before use in order to remove the excessive saltiness.

Mountain villages in Cyprus.

BRINJAL BAKE
with tomatoes and capers

3 medium brinjals (aubergines)
3 ripe medium tomatoes, skinned and chopped
75 ml olive oil
40 ml pickled capers, drained
45 ml chopped fresh basil
1 clove garlic, crushed
a few grindings of black pepper
125 ml dry breadcrumbs

Preheat the oven to 180 °C.

Slice the brinjals (±2 cm) lengthways. To pre-cook the brinjals, heat a ridged grilling pan well and grill them, approximately 5 minutes on each side. They do not need to be fully cooked at this stage. (If you do not have a grilling pan, you could fry them in a little olive oil in a frying pan.)

Combine the tomatoes, olive oil, capers, basil, garlic and black pepper.

Oil a shallow ovenproof dish large enough to arrange the brinjal slices in a single layer and pack them tightly against one another. Spread the tomato-caper mixture over the slices and finish off with a sprinkling of breadcrumbs.

Bake for 45 minutes. Test to ensure that the brinjals are cooked through and tender. If not, bake a little longer. The topping should be deliciously brown; if not, pop under the grill for a few minutes.

This dish is mouthwatering as it comes out of the oven, but if left for a day, the flavours will develop even further. Serve at room temperature with a drizzle of olive oil and flatbread. Pure ambrosia! Serves 4 as a light meal

CAPER AND YOGHURT SAUCE

Mediteranean people seem to have a million delectable sauces and dips ranging from mayonnaise to mashed potato, bean paste to baba ghanoush. The following is a caper-flavoured, mock mayonnaise.

75 g stale white bread
75 g pickled capers
a generous handful of Italian flat-leaf parsley, roughly chopped
4–5 spring onions (with green parts), roughly chopped
1 clove garlic, roughly chopped
2 egg yolks
150 ml extra virgin olive oil
150 ml very thick Greek yoghurt
salt and pepper to taste

Soak the bread in water, then squeeze dry. Place in a food processor with the capers, parsley, spring onions and garlic, and blend well.

Add the egg yolks and blend briefly. While the motor is still running, add the olive oil a little at a time. Stir in the yoghurt and season to taste.

Serve chilled or at room temperature, with potatoes, boiled eggs, fish or grilled vegetables. Makes ±500 ml

GOOD IDEAS FOR CAPER COMBINATIONS

- A quartet of smoked salmon, capers, potatoes and a lemon dressing is heavenly.
- A caper berry served with an egg mousse and topped with croutons, delicious!
- Crisply fried capers with sizzling olive oil poured over poached white fish gives the dish a Mediterranean touch.

He Put in his
Thumb and
Pulled out
a Plum

Villa Athena offers self-catering apartments based on the Greek vernacular and with Greek-style interiors. Each unit has a small kitchen nook where one may prepare easy summer meals with the greatest of ease. Sitting on the apartment balcony with the view of the Aegean beyond turns even the simplest meal into a king's feast.

Our guests would, from time to time, arrive late at night or early in the morning. In such an event, we stocked the kitchen with a few breakfast delicacies or invited them to a welcome breakfast on the terrace of the main house.

My special friendship with Yannis brought special benefits. We often strolled past his orchard and I was intrigued by some plum trees bearing fruit that might have been taken straight from an old master's painting. The plums were longish and oval, with little cheeks. As they ripened, their red colour deepened and a white bloom formed while they peeped temptingly from behind a screen of elegantly curved leaves. A genuine enquiry as to the variety of plum and the fact that I admired the vast crop created magic! I was told that they were Damascus plums, the trees were only lightly pruned because they were still quite young and that they had had a good composting that winter, which, in addition to a good spring watering, produced a crop beyond expectation. If I liked, I was invited to pick some. Carefully. And with the promise that I would produce some *marmelatha* (jam).

So it came to pass that our guests would sit on our terrace to enjoy their welcome breakfast of hot croissants, feta cheese and generous bowls of thick, fat Greek yoghurt liberally stained with freshly poached Damascus plums oozing magenta liquid. In their kitchen a bottle of ruby-red plum jam awaited them for the following day's breakfast on their own balcony.

Villa Athena takes its name from the goddess Athena, daughter of Zeus, king of the ancient Greek gods, who sent lightning and thunderbolts to earth to remind the mortals of his supreme power over the heavens.

Athena was born fully armed from her father's head and was worshipped for her gift of wisdom and her skills in the tasks of daily life. She was also the goddess of oxen, horses and olives. Many temples were dedicated to Athena, in particular the temple on the Acropolis in Athens. She was a perpetual virgin and according to legend, she blinded Tiresias for seeing her naked.

HE PUT IN HIS THUMB AND PULLED OUT A PLUM

STEWED FRESH PLUMS

I have no problems with Greeks bearing gifts. The Damascus plums from Yannis's own trees brought a number of people much happiness! In the event of a glut of something, my mind starts to race; how can I preserve some of this to prolong the enjoyment? I stewed and stewed …

1 kg plums, stoned
250 ml sugar

Place the plums into an ample saucepan. Add the sugar. Leave this to stand a while. The sugar will draw the juices and will start dissolving.

Over a gentle heat, stir the plums until it is apparent that all the sugar has dissolved. Only then increase the heat and stew the plums until they are cooked through – this will take about 8 minutes.

Pour into sterilised, warm glass jars, seal immediately and leave to cool.

While the simplicity of the plain plums appeals to me, I have not been above popping the odd piece of cinnamon stick, vanilla pod or a splash of Metaxa brandy into the jars just before I seal them. These jars of plums will last very well in a refrigerator, but must not be viewed as similar to highly sugared jams and butters that can last for years on a pantry shelf!

Enjoy the stewed plums with thick Greek yoghurt, mixed into smoothies or as a substitute for fresh plums in cakes or tarts. Makes 2 x 250 ml jars

Damascus plums and figs from Yannis Mitzelos's trees on Skiathos (opposite).

PLUM AND FRANGIPANI TART

PASTRY
150 g butter
300 g cake flour
1 egg, lightly beaten

FILLING
150 g butter
150 g sugar
2 eggs
130 g ground almonds
35 g cake flour
500 g fresh plums, halved and stoned

Grease a 30-cm loose-bottomed cake tin.

To make the pastry, rub the butter into the flour until it resembles fine crumbs. Mix in the egg and shape the dough into a ball. If necessary, add a drop of water. The texture should be firm but not dry, tending towards 'short' or crumbly. Wrap in clingfilm and chill in the refrigerator for 30 minutes. Preheat the oven to 180 °C.

Roll out the pastry on a floured surface, then line the cake tin with it. Blind bake for 15 minutes. Leave to cool.

For the filling, cream the butter and sugar well before adding the eggs, one at a time. Beat well. Stir in the almonds and the flour.

Spoon this mixture into the baked shell and arrange the plums on top. Bake in the oven for 55 minutes at 180 °C or until the filling rises and is golden brown.

HE PUT IN HIS THUMB AND PULLED OUT A PLUM

Poppies, Nettles and Dandelions

Poppies in May on a beach on Skopelos Island, Greece.

Growing up with a wealth of illustrated children's books, it was apparent that no child's world existed without a landscape of toadstools, poppies, nettles, dandelions, candy-tufts, buttercups, snowdrops and a variety of beautiful weeds. Our parents dutifully instructed us about the pretty but poisonous plants, which we fearfully avoided – along with other 'horrors'. So sound was this education that we shunned all the delightful edible plants until, as adults, we discovered their enchantments.

$\mathscr{D}$ANDELIONS

On a sunny Sunday many years ago we went walking on the mountainside in Constantia. In our group was a new friend: Michaelis – Greek, handsome, talented, kind and down-to-earth. He constantly stooped to uproot young dandelion plants. This was the first time I realised they were edible! He rinsed them well, removed only the yellowing or damaged leaves, before blanching them in a few drops of olive oil. Arranged on a plate, roots and all, they had lemon squeezed over them, a little salt and pepper ground onto them to become a delightful salad; slightly bitter, with the sweetness of ripe tomatoes and the nuttiness of roast beetroot … mmmmmmmm.

In the early 1980s I lectured at the Cape Town Teachers' Training College in the evenings; this after running morning and afternoon classes at two schools. In between I needed food! My search led me to a small bakery run by an affable Greek and his shy wife. *Baklava, tiropitas, spanakopitas*, custard slices and baguettes became my staples, deliciously fresh and tempting. Hard work was rewarded when the owners moved to larger premises, from which they also ran a small Greek restaurant. We became regular diners. One evening, in a fit of spontaneity, Kyria Maria offered us some of the family's own salad – a plate of freshly picked dandelion plants (with roots) in olive oil, served with lemon wedges. Knowing the care and time bestowed upon the dish, we were overcome. Those little dandelions saw the start of a very special, slightly reserved friendship. Growing ever larger, the bakery moved again, and again, sadly losing the dandelions, mountain mushrooms and other things that matter!

$\mathscr{N}$ETTLES

My grandfather's mules were beautiful. Workers they were, four of them pulling a cart laden with freshly harvested tomatoes or crisp green lettuce, parsnips, carrots, swedes and turnips. In turn, they were used to drag the plough or the *eg* (harrow). Their paddocks near the farmstead were used in rotation – sometimes sown with lucerne, sometimes lying fallow and in between used for grazing. The wild flowers, weeds, odd poppy or nasturtium would thrive there in winter. And nettles! The most beautiful, lush, well-nourished green nettles, waist high and fine mule food. Only now

do I realise how we missed out on beautiful green soups, risottos and salads. Instead we broke off long stems and whacked one another's bare legs. Wicked, heartless children.

As winter settled in towards the end of May 2009, we prepared to leave the town of Franschhoek and move back to our home in Cape Town. Walking through the bare pear orchards across a carpet of mossy green grass, it was evident that the areas around the trees had been fertilised. Those were the spots where common daisies, thistles and nettles seemed to flourish. Memories of the mule paddocks came to mind and while I could still feel my shins stinging, the nettles conjured up visions of bowls of piping hot soup.

I had to wear a pair of unattractive, yellow household gloves to harvest the nettles, learning as I went: new shoots are more desirable, the gloves need to cover one's wrists, and some of the sturdy leaves can sting right through thin gloves. However, I quickly collected enough for a large serving.

Back home, still wearing the gloves, I rinsed the harvest well, picked out any bad parts, discarded thick stems and shook handfuls of leaves to lose most of the water. I then dropped them into a large saucepan and poured boiling water over the nettles; this put paid to their sting! Once they were totally wilted (but still beautifully green), I drained and squeezed as much water out of them as possible. At this point I could freeze them, chop them up roughly for soup or very finely for a risotto. I do not like to freeze foods, but with the nettles being so seasonal I succumbed.

$\mathcal{P}$OPPIES

The poppies of Flanders … a spot of red on a lapel to remember war heroes. This was my first memory of poppies. My aunt Hester grew poppies in her garden, but they were big, double and much grander than the simple red ones I preferred. Nonetheless, I grew up discovering more and more poppies … Californian, Iceland … I love them all.

In the garden of Villa Athena on the island of Skiathos, Veron, our dear Albanian friend and I cleared a patch for vegetables. Sadly, we had to pull up many little poppy plants. It was early in the season and they were too young to flower. Veron kept every poppy plant, explaining that they were intended for a salad. At lunchtime he rinsed the plants but kept the roots intact.

Veron and I trying to retrieve the water pump in the well at Villa Athena, Skiathos.

While we sliced tomatoes, cucumber, fresh bread and feta cheese, Veron warmed a drop of fragrant olive oil in a large saucepan. He shook the water off the seedlings and dropped them into the hot saucepan. He turned the flame off and shook the poppies about. Within minutes they were wilted, but luminously green. Spread out on a platter they looked intriguing. A drizzle of fresh olive oil, a squeeze of lemon, salt and ground black pepper finished it off. The resultant luncheon was memorable: made with love, unexpected, new and delicious. Slightly bitter, not over-cooked or too soft, but neither raw nor too crispy.

NETTLE AND ROASTED PEAR SOUP

1 small onion, chopped
30 ml butter
2 carrots, chopped
1 stick celery, sliced
1 fat leek, sliced
1 litre water
1 large potato, cubed
500 g fresh nettle tips or young shoots, chopped
salt and pepper
1 ripe but firm pear, peeled and cored
a sprinkling of brown sugar

In a saucepan, fry the onion in 1 tablespoon (15 ml) of butter until translucent, but not darkened. Add the carrots, celery, leek and water. Bring to the boil and simmer for 30 minutes. Remove from the heat and strain. Discard the vegetables and return the stock to the saucepan. Add the potato and boil until it is soft. Finally, add the nettles while the stock is still boiling and cook, uncovered, for 15 minutes.

Remove from the heat and leave to cool slightly before blending the soup. Season with salt and pepper. Keep warm but do not allow to boil again.

Cut the pear lengthways, arranging the slices on a baking tray. Sprinkle with sugar and dot with the remaining butter. Place under a hot grill until they start to brown.

Serve the soup with a few slices of grilled pear. For a richer dish, place a dollop of sour cream or crème fraîche over the pear slices. Serves 4 as a starter

A citrus vendor in Fez, Morocco.

Oranges and Lemons

The stall of a citrus juice seller in the Djemâa el-Fna square in Marrakech.

Oranges at school … When I was little, school lunches were the order of the day. Glasses of milk, apples, chunks of cheese, margarine sandwiches on Government brown bread (enriched with fish meal!) and, just when our moist little winter-noses needed it most, sweet oranges stamped 'OUTSPAN'.

Over time we got to know our oranges. There were those with thin skins and many pips. Preparing them for consumption involved discreet underfoot-rolling until they were marshmallow soft and (to adults) totally disgusting. A good wash under running tap water was advised, yet we frequently persuaded everybody concerned that a good wipe with the end of a school shirt would suffice. At this point you had to summon up the courage to bite into the top of the fruit, peeling away just enough rind to allow your index finger to penetrate the flesh. This bite left a bitter, burning taste, stinging your lips, especially in the little winter cracks, and caused an anethesia that lasted too long. But the reward was the first draught of sweet juice – and a pip. Squeezing, sucking, spitting pips. A crooked finger delved into the pithy depths of an orange, churning it about, loosening the cells, undoing the segments. First prize was to remove all the insides with the shell intact. Some oranges had to be torn open, turned inside out and nibbled clean of all flesh. Our sore, burny mouths were quite forgotten by the time we bit into the next orange.

Thick-skinned oranges were a different matter altogether. They could not be rolled, squeezed or churned, but had to be tackled in the Mom-prescribed manner: peeled with (grubby) fingers, thumbs forced into the top to tear segments apart, and eaten bit by bit. Like a gentleman.

Strangely though, this fancy method left us with dirty-brown orange segments, juicy palms and wrists, and frequently spotty clothes. But our lips were not numb.

Sipping fresh orange juice in Lefkara in Cyprus.

THE TROMPSBURG ORANGE ADVENTURE

I grew up on a farm, in Retreat, just a 30-minute train ride from the city centre of Cape Town. A child of the *platteland* (rural countryside) and the city in one!

Winter holidays were spent visiting family and friends in the Karoo, Free State and further north, to escape the wet Cape winters. When I was about 11, we holidayed on a farm in the Trompsburg area of the Free State. The food was delicious, the beds feathery and snug, the fires fascinating, the farm animals tame, approachable and intriguing. But I was not sure about the children. They kindly showed me how to warm my feet (we were always barefoot) by wiggling my toes into a fresh cow-pat. Was this kind of them or wicked? The 12 year old – sporting a farm vehicle driver's licence – drove us to the orange grove and honoured me by allowing me to open the farm gate, whereupon they drove off without me. To a city boy the Free State was vast, desolate and frightening, standing there alone and 'abandoned'. They did come back for me a while later and we went to pick oranges. What fun they had laughing at the silly, gullible city boy!

The oranges were intended mainly for a baked dessert that evening. With so many mouths to feed – particularly those of growing boys – Aunt Emily prepared a dish of mammoth proportions. The delicious, slightly tart but sweet pudding baked into a light, cake-like top layer over a runny sauce. On the farm we had a dollop of fresh cream with each helping. The city dweller in me believes this is overkill though.

My orange experiences did not end with the lovely dessert. Games followed. The adults played cards in the sitting room and the children gathered in the cosy kitchen. I tried to be invisible in the sitting room while much giggling and *sotto voce* nattering emanated from the kitchen. My aunt suggested I join the kitchen gang and I obviously could not disobey. They welcomed me a little too enthusiastically.

'We're playing donkey.' Fine.

'But not pinning on the tail.' Relief.

'You must wear a blindfold.' Oh no!

'Point your finger and keep it firm.'

There was a donkey on the table in front of me. A little brother on all fours. 'You tell us on which part of the donkey we are placing your finger now? Hold your finger stiff!'

I felt a nose. 'Nose!' Then an ear. 'Ear.' Neck. 'Neck?' Back. 'Back.' Hind leg. 'Hind leg.' Buttocks. 'Buttocks!?'

'Hold your finger STIFF!' Panic attack.

My finger went into something warm, soft, moist, disgusting, nauseating … citrus.

To prepare this thin-skinned orange for childish enjoyment, warm it in the drawer of an Aga while blindfolding an unsuspecting victim.

The terrace at the Marriott Hotel in Zamelek, Cairo.

LES CITRONS PRESSES

It was not summer, but the sun beat down mercilessly. The busyness of Cairo got to us and we searched for an oasis. This we found in the courtyard of the Cairo Marriott Hotel. Umbrella-shaded tables flanked a walkway that served as an early evening promenade and a course for the ever-running waiters. Strolling up and down were Saudi businessmen in their crisp white garments, bored Cairene mothers in stylish outfits reining in their children, French tourists reciting the dynasties, Germans being briefed by their guide …

'Two citrons presses, please.' They arrived: frosted glasses of pale green liquid with a topping of ice crystals. As usual, I added some fine sugar, Lennie sprinkled some salt into his glass. With puckering mouths we sipped the most delicious drink for a hot summer afternoon.

LEMON CAKE

90 g butter
210 g castor sugar
2 eggs, lightly beaten
200 g self-raising flour, sifted
a pinch of salt
125 ml milk
juice and zest of 1 lemon
150 g white sugar

Preheat the oven to 180 °C. Grease a 23-cm cake tin or a 12-cup cupcake pan.

Cream the butter and castor sugar well together. Whisk the eggs into the creamed butter until it is very pale in colour and light in texture.

Fold the flour and salt into the mixture, bit by bit, alternating with the milk. Spoon into the cake tin, then bake for about 25 minutes (or 20 minutes if using a cupcake pan). Test with a skewer for doneness.

Combine the lemon juice and zest with the white sugar in a saucepan. Dissolve over a gentle heat, then bring to the boil for about 4 minutes.

Turn the cake (or individual cakes) out when ready and prick all over before drenching with the syrup while still warm.
Serves 6

ORANGE AND FENNEL SALAD
with pickled lemon dressing

1 cos lettuce
3 oranges
2 medium fennel bulbs

DRESSING
50 ml virgin olive oil
juice of 1 lemon
5–7 ml honey
pickled lemon rind (see p. 170), finely
  diced, to taste
salt and freshly ground black pepper
  to taste

Rinse and dry the cos lettuce leaves and arrange them in a salad bowl.

Peel the oranges deep enough to reveal the flesh and neatly cut the wedges free from the pith. (Reserve any juice that oozes out.) Slice the fennel bulbs thinly, crossways, and reserve some of the 'fronds' for garnishing.

To make the dressing, mix the olive oil, lemon juice and honey, and whisk to an emulsion. Add the lemon rind. As these are salty, first taste before adding additional seasoning salt. Grind some black pepper into the dressing.

Macerate the orange segments and fennel slices in a little dressing and toss together. Arrange over the lettuce leaves and garnish with the reserved fennel 'fronds'. Serves 4 as a starter or as a side dish.

One Potato,
Two Potato,
Three Potato,
... More

Ever since I can remember, I have liked potatoes.

Grandpa's kitchen (Grandma died very long ago) was large, with a number of staff who cooked, cleaned, polished and washed dishes. But Johanna was my favourite, mainly, I suppose, because she saved the tastiest morsels for me. She always prepared the most glorious dish of potatoes for Sunday lunch. It was very much a family affair, with extended tables accommodating the entire family. There were wine glasses at every place setting. Large glasses for the adults and thimble-sized ones for the children.

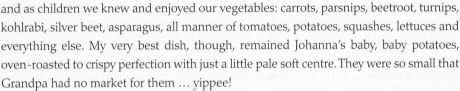

Lamb, chicken and beef were served with an array of seasonal vegetables. Grandpa was a vegetable farmer and as children we knew and enjoyed our vegetables: carrots, parsnips, beetroot, turnips, kohlrabi, silver beet, asparagus, all manner of tomatoes, potatoes, squashes, lettuces and everything else. My very best dish, though, remained Johanna's baby, baby potatoes, oven-roasted to crispy perfection with just a little pale soft centre. They were so small that Grandpa had no market for them … yippee!

When we reached the stage at school when our teacher asked us to bring potatoes – big ones – for making potato prints, Grandpa sponsored an entire pocket. My love for potatoes was firmly cemented by those potato print classes. I knew instinctively to carve the images back to front. And my repeat patterns always registered. Sort of.

―――※※※―――

In my experience the most delicious potatoes in the entire world come from the red soil of the eastern parts of Cyprus. The idea of baked potatoes in Greece sounded incongruous to me. Oven-baked with rosemary, olive oil and coarse salt, yes, but *sketo* (plain) oven-baked, no! However … they arrived at the table, larger than most, with a magical crisp leather skin and piping hot. When I cut a cross into its tummy it revealed a rich, almost saffron-yellow, soft, creamy inside. I poured a line of golden green olive oil into the cuts and crushed pure white feta into them as well. Thick slices of sun-ripened tomatoes and salty black olives rounded off the luncheon. Until then I never realised that potatoes could have such an earthy, intense flavour.

―――※※※―――

In her book *The Glorious Foods of Greece*, Diane Kochilas refers to *skordalia* as a 'cult status' dish in Cephalonia. It is a garlic sauce, bread- or potato-based, sometimes enhanced with ground almonds or walnuts. A little lemon juice or white wine vinegar adds piquancy while some recipes call for an egg yolk to create a mayonnaise taste. The olive oil component is a given. *Skordalia* is often served as an accompaniment to little fish balls, meats or even salads, a favourite in Cephalonia being a salad of wilted vine shoots and olive oil. Only the newest three leaves and tendrils at the end of spring shoots are considered suitable.

SKORDALIA

500 g potatoes (a floury variety if possible)
6 (or more) cloves garlic, to taste
400–500 ml extra virgin olive oil
a generous squeeze of lemon juice or a splash of white wine vinegar
75 g almonds or walnuts, finely ground (optional)

Boil the potatoes in their skins in salted water until soft. Leave to cool, then peel them. Mash very smoothly. (A ricer works best for this, but if you don't have one, press through a sieve.) Using a mortar and pestle or a food processor, reduce the garlic to a smooth paste, then add it to the mashed potatoes. Work the olive oil into the mixture, little by little, also adding the lemon juice or vinegar. The final sauce should be quite thick and definitely not runny. It is not advisable to make the entire sauce in a mixer or processor as the potatoes could easily turn into a gooey mess.

Finally, if you like, mix through some almonds or walnuts. Serves 6 as a starter with fingers of crisp bread

Greco-Roman Fayoum portrait. One still sees this type of face in Egypt today.

POTATOES
wrapped in phyllo pastry

This appetiser recipe was inspired by the mezze *at Anatoli, a Turkish restaurant in Cape Town, which celebrated its 25th anniversary in 2009. Established all those years ago by Bevan Christie, it has remained essentially Turkish and is now in the hands of Tayfun Aras, himself a Turk.*

500 g potatoes
a knob of butter
a splash of olive oil
1 medium onion, finely chopped
2 large eggs
10 ml milk
200 ml grated Kefalotiri or Pecorino cheese
a few sprigs of flat-leaf parsley, chopped
1 red chilli, deseeded and finely chopped
100 g butter
500 g phyllo pastry
paprika

Boil the potatoes in their jackets, in salted water, until soft. Heat the knob of butter and the olive oil in a pan and fry the onion until soft, but still pale. Peel the potatoes, then mash them. Add the onion and mix in well. Beat the eggs lightly and mix into the potatoes along with the milk, cheese, parsley and chilli. Chill in the refrigerator.

Melt the 100 g of butter. Spread the phyllo pastry sheets out and cover them with a slightly moist cloth while working with individual sheets. Lay 4 sheets of pastry widthways on your work surface, then cut them in half from top to bottom. Stack them (8 halves) on top of one other. Place another sheet of pastry next to the stack and brush it liberally with the melted butter. Remove the potato filling from the refrigerator and pile it along the edge of the buttered pastry, forming it into a 'sausage' along the full width. Roll the 'sausage' in the pastry. Butter the next sheet of phyllo and wrap another layer around the 'potato sausage'. Continue until all the sheets have been used. Wrap the entire potato-phyllo log in clingwrap and chill again.

Preheat the oven to 180 °C. Using a sharp knife, cut the chilled log into 2-cm wheels. Arrange on a baking tray and brush liberally with more butter. Dust with a little paprika and bake for approximately 30 minutes, until golden.

Enjoy while hot, perhaps with a tomato coulis. Serves 6 as a starter

$\mathscr{P}$OTATO SALAD

I have been making this potato salad for ages, but spontaneously rather than from a recipe.

I suppose it started with Tante Edith, a German woman my uncle married. She introduced us to the mayonnaise-less potato salad – a great novelty in the 1950s. Her recipe was distinctly German, with chopped onion, chopped parsley and finally, after adding a splash of vinegar, a generous quantity of really crispy bacon, with the fat from the frying pan added in for good measure. Cholesterol had not been 'invented' yet as a health problem!

As I became increasingly partial to things Mediterranean, the German salad became Greek. The basics remained the same: potatoes, onion, olive oil and parsley, but it was red onion, extra virgin olive oil and flat-leaf parsley (in abundance!). Sometimes I also add olives, capers, bits of red pepper, sumac and dukkah.

500 g new potatoes
50 ml cumin seeds
60 ml virgin olive oil
30 ml lemon juice
cayenne pepper to taste
10 black olives, pitted (optional)
1 bunch flat-leaf parsley, chopped
1 small red onion, thinly sliced
a sprinkling of paprika

Boil the potatoes in their skins, in salted water, until soft. Titchy ones may be left as is, but larger ones could be halved or quartered. It is a matter of taste, but I prefer them with their skins intact.

Heat the cumin seeds in a little frying pan and toast briefly, then grind them using a mortar and pestle.

Prepare the dressing by mixing the oil, lemon juice, ground cumin and cayenne pepper. Pour it over the still-hot potatoes and sprinkle the olives, parsley and onion slices over them. Turn the potatoes well to drench them in the dressing and for the flavours to meld. Finally, add a tasty and decorative shake of paprika over the dish before serving. Serves 6 as a side dish

Wooden houses in Istanbul, circa 1970 (left), a seaside locanda (tavern) along the Bosphorus, Turkey (below), and the imposing Agia Sofia, Istanbul (opposite).

Humpty Dumpty

My earliest memory of eggs? Soft-boiled eggs with toast fingers. This was not only breakfast, it was an adventure! In our household you had your own egg cup. Mine was a chubby creamware elephant, while the toast plate was celadon.

Eating a boiled egg on my own was not as much fun as sitting at the breakfast table with Grandpa. He would chop off the top of my egg in a mighty swoop and I could scoop the white out of the severed top. A tiny quantity of fine salt was deposited on my saucer; I was old enough to sprinkle a few grains onto my egg. I churned the egg a little with my spoon until the yellow threatened to spill. At this point I mustered the soldiers: narrow fingers of buttered wholewheat toast. Carefully I loaded the first soldier with some yellow, some white … moved forward and marched it into my wide-open mouth. Not a drop spilled. As soon as there was space inside the egg, the soldiers were dunked, thereafter to carry the delightful runny mess to my mouth. The ritual did not stop at an empty shell. Wicked witches rowed across the river in empty shells, or so we were told! So, each shell was punctured for safety – even Grandpa's!

The creamware elephant egg cup of my childhood.

ℬREAKFAST AT THE PUDDING SHOP

In 1970, I think it was about mid-August, Charlotte du Toit, who worked at the South African Embassy in Athens, invited us for a glass of *retsina* (wine flavoured with pine resin). She introduced us to a delightful group of Canadians and an Englishman. We discovered that we were all on our way to Istanbul; ourselves travelling through Greece and they crossing to Turkey and then travelling north along the Turkish coast.

'Let's meet on Friday at the Pudding Shop,' suggested the Englishman.

We queried its location and he recommended that we drive to the Blue Mosque, park and ask for directions. On the appointed Friday we arrived at the Blue Mosque, dutifully parked and requested directions.

'Right there,' we were told sharply.

Our new friends were not there but, hungry, we sat down for breakfast. Swayed by the fare on the tables around us we ordered the Turkish egg dish. Each of us was presented with a small metal pan with two handles. On a base of fragrant tomato sauce lay two eggs, cooked to perfection. A stack of pitas was soon reduced to a few crumbs as we scooped up red piquant sauce with islands of white and streaks of bright yellow.

While enjoying our breakfast we saw a notice board covered with intriguing notelets of all sizes, hues and scripts. For a few cents one could post a message: 'Two Germans travelling to Kabul looking for two lady companions' …'Lonely girl seeking English tutor' … and one from our new Canadian friends … looking for us!

*A*NYONE FOR TENNIS?

Tennis parties in the 1950s to me meant left-over rainbow sandwiches with fillings of watercress, cucumber, egg-mayonnaise and egg-and-tomato mayonnaise. (I also seem to remember the fuss about Gussie Moran's frilly underwear showing at Wimbledon.)

Back to eggs though. I really didn't mind helping my Mom and the other tennis ladies in the kitchen as I could taste every single left-over in the course of an afternoon. It followed that these tennis players competed not only on court, but also in the kitchen. Your popularity at the tennis club was directly linked to fleet-footedness on court, your social skills (especially being a jolly loser), pretty outfits and delectable treats at teatime. Some dashing dressers with excellent social skills (attested to by all the gentlemen players), but miraculous abilities to miss the balls driven straight at them, also seemed to fail dismally in the kitchen department. Their failures ranged from simply forgetting the goodies in the refrigerator at home to 'sarmies' that were too thick, or sour cream with scones.

My measure was always the egg-mayonnaise sandwich fillings. I liked a creamy consistency without too many bits of unmashed egg white. The mayonnaise thing was sometimes overdone and I did not care for that, nor did I enjoy little surprises of chopped gherkin in the mixture. It was, after all, an 'eggy' treat. I made such a fuss of Mrs Naude's sandwiches that she said that she would like to adopt me. This was a very attractive notion given her prowess as cook and baker! Sadly, her little figure supported by size 3 tennis shoes did not quite make the grade on the court.

Other party pieces of the '50s and '60s were various egg mousses, *oeufs en gelée* and stuffed eggs! Robert Carrier was a star in the firmament of English chefs. His wonderfully detailed guidelines, intimate knowledge and understanding of food, the kitchen and presentation never failed to fascinate me. In today's world of extraordinary fusions and pairings, his choices might be considered staid, boring or too conservative, but I maintain that classical marriages of egg and anchovy, egg and cucumber, egg and mayonnaise, egg and avocado, and egg and caviar can't be bettered. Carrier favoured the following fillings for hard-boiled eggs: anchovy and parsley, avocado and green pepper, and chutney. The following are my own recipes for these fillings. In each instance, use four hard-boiled eggs, halved lengthways and yolks removed.

Old Turkish postcards. Note the Agia Sofia (below), still as a mosque, pre-1934, in Istanbul.

TUFFED EGGS

ANCHOVY AND PARSLEY STUFFING

Place 4 hardboiled egg yolks, 125 ml mayonnaise, about 45 ml very finely chopped parsley and 15 ml anchovy essence (or 2 small anchovies, rinsed and finely chopped) in a bowl. Mash to a smooth paste.

AVOCADO AND GREEN PEPPER STUFFING

Mash together 4 hardboiled egg yolks, the flesh of 1 medium avocado, 30 ml mayonnaise, 30 ml lemon juice and some crushed garlic to taste. Mix in 15 ml spring onion and 15 ml green pepper, both very finely chopped.

CHUTNEY STUFFING

This stuffing reminds me of the old-fashioned (and not universally popular) dish of curried eggs and fluffy rice. Mash together 4 hardboiled egg yolks, 60 ml mayonnaise, 3 ml good quality curry powder, 60 ml chutney, 45 ml finely chopped parsley and a dash of cayenne pepper.

In each instance, spoon the filling into the egg white cavities, each generously mounded, and garnish appropriately.

Flakes of *nori* (seaweed) look good with the anchovy eggs, as will a single caper berry on each avocado egg and a sprig of fresh coriander on the chutney eggs.

I certainly do not see these as finger food, the way they used to be served (as you invariably ended up with stuffed fingers as well), but as a luncheon with crisp green salad leaves, bright red tomatoes and a free-for-all supply of crusty bread – as well as civilised knives and forks! As each of these stuffings is sufficient for 4 eggs, you must decide how many to prepare per person as a starter or a light lunch.

$\mathcal{M}$ENEMEN

In Turkey we enjoyed the breakfast dish of eggs and tomato, known as Menemen, *served in individual small frying pans. The Tunisians and Moroccans offer a similar dish called* chakchouka. *With their addition of harissa, it could be quite a fiery breakfast or brunch!*

2 large green peppers, deseeded and sliced
2 large onions, sliced
olive oil for braising
2 x 400 g cans chopped tomatoes
salt and freshly ground black pepper
harissa to taste (optional)
6 eggs

Preheat the oven to 180 °C.

In a saucepan, braise the peppers and onions in the olive oil until quite tender. Mix in the tomatoes and simmer until the mixture becomes a rich, homogenous sauce. Add salt and pepper to taste. At this point, you could also add the 'fire' of some harissa – if that is to your taste.

Spoon the mixture into 6 small ovenproof dishes. Break an egg on top of each. Bake in the oven until the eggs are set, but not hard.

Serve with a little stack of flatbreads, extra harissa and some thick yoghurt. Serves 6

Examples of ancient Italian stone carvings.

Peter, Peter, Pumpkin Eater

'At the stroke of twelve, the coach turned into a pumpkin …'

I'll bet that Cinderella developed a slight resistance to pumpkin after that little episode!

Pumpkin, butternut, squash, courgette and marrow count among my favourite vegetables. Strangely, but probably because of their seasonality, they are considered ingredients for winter dishes. And yet they can successfully be part of a summer salad or a summer supper of fritters, salsa and crème fraîche.

A view of farraglioni rock formations from the island of Capri.

A lovely recipe for a pumpkin *bredie* (a typical Cape stew) was given to me by a delightful friend, Edna Helfet. A girl from Namaqualand, she was a natural cook and gourmet – in addition to having a charming personality and the most beautiful sparkling eyes and red-lipped smile. I pass it on unchanged. At the time we used to joke about the lovely old *boerpampoene* (farm pumpkins), which would last for ages languishing on the corrugated iron roofs of the ubiquitous outhouses at the end of the garden.

To dispel the legend of the winteriness of butternut, I sometimes serve a curious salad of grated carrot, grated raw butternut, lentils, coriander, ginger and cumin. Made a little in advance, the flavours meld to bring to mind a North African taste experience.

Gem squashes mean baby food to many people. Well, I love this baby food. Steamed to squashy perfection, filled with fresh peas and topped with a pat of butter and grated nutmeg, it is old-fashioned, pedestrian, non-U and, in my mind, a dish fit for a king!

The most delicious wintry soup that I have ever eaten was served by Fiamma Swainston at her lovely restaurant in Wynberg. It beggared experimentation and I would like to offer my version of this rich and flavoursome mushroom soup served in half a gem squash. It is rich and simple, textured and creamy – what a combination!

It is alarming that foods also are subjected to whims, fashions and reputations. I doubt that most young people these days even know what a real grown-up marrow is. One of my childhood favourites was a large marrow stuffed with spicy meat and baked in the oven. The resulting sauce was thickened with flour and butter. Slices of this delicacy served on a heavy white plate, napped with whitish gravy and served with carrots and whole young peas might sound mundane, but it always cheered our family.

Baby marrows, however, are commonplace nowadays. Also known by their foreign names 'zucchini' and 'courgettes', they are ever popular, especially in Mediterranean cuisine. Raw, cut into matchsticks and added to a salad they reveal their basic flavour. Fractionally richer is a steamed version served topped with butter and nutmeg. They are an integral part of the lovely French ratatouille, while in Greece they are battered and deep-fried. Grilled in a ridged pan, thin slices acquire lovely dark lines. I moisten them with olive oil, sprinkle them with chopped parsley and serve them as a *mezze*.

The most exquisite dish with baby marrows does, in fact, not concern the vegetable as much as the flower. We once wandered along the pathways of Capri. Up and down we went, thankful for the occasional level stretch. We had just been trespassing in order to view the Villa Fehrsen, which at the time was being restored. Our Canadian friends Irene and Philip led the expedition and were not deterred by a mere 'Keep Out' sign and a locked gate. Philip's ten Italian words and tons of charm not only gained us entry, but we were also ushered around by the various craftsmen – plasterers, sculptors, mosaicists, gilders, decorative painters and carvers – who filled us in on the fascinating history of the house. Some of the workers were setting up for lunch under the pine trees and the sight and fragrance of their midday meal prompted us to find a *trattoria* immediately!

As luck would have it, we found just the right place – a little restaurant set in the garden of a very ordinary-looking house. Our table was under a pergola of vines heavy with bunches of grapes. The vegetable garden stretched down to the road and the abundance astounded us. There were tomatoes, peppers, sweet basil, zucchini and herbs of every kind. The patrons were mostly locals, and the family of mother, father and daughter who ran the establishment could speak no English. Their personal involvement, however, was evident in the quality, variety, preparation and service of the lunch. Their trump card that afternoon was stuffed zucchini flowers! Now, years later, we can still recall our first-ever taste of those sublime morsels. Of course, the rest of the meal was delicious and the wine delightful, but those delicate yellow flowers folded around a rice stuffing … ambrosia!

A pathway in Capri (top), the Villa Fehrsen ballroom (centre),
and restoration of Villa Fehrsen in progress, 1994 (bottom).

EDNA HELFET'S SPICY PUMPKIN BREDIE

30 ml sunflower oil

4 onions, sliced

1 kg lean stewing lamb or veal, cubed

250 ml water

1 large piece of fresh ginger

1 roll stick cinnamon

4 whole cloves

3 cloves garlic, peeled

30 ml white sugar

salt and freshly ground black pepper to taste

1.5 kg pumpkin, peeled and coarsely cubed

2–3 fresh red chillies

± 1 litre good vegetable or beef stock or white wine

Preheat the oven to 160 °C.

In a large ovenproof casserole, heat the oil then brown the onions on the stovetop. First remove the onions then brown the meat in the same pot. Add the onions again.

Add the 250 ml water and bring to a gentle simmer. In the meanwhile, pound the ginger, cinnamon, cloves, garlic, sugar and salt in a mortar. Add the spice mixture to the meat, season with pepper and cover.

Bake in the oven for 1 hour. Add the pumpkin pieces and chillies, as well as a little of the stock or white wine. Cover and return to the oven for another hour. From time to time, add the remainder of the stock or wine.

Serve with *borrie* rice (rice flavoured with turmeric). Serves 6 as a main course

SOUP IN A GEM SQUASH

4 gem squash with hard skin
50 g dried shiitake mushrooms
30 ml sunflower oil
15 ml butter
1 medium red onion, chopped
500 g brown mushrooms, cubed
1 medium potato, peeled and cubed
750 ml vegetable stock
a few drops of truffle oil
salt and freshly ground black pepper to taste
a little mashed potato for serving

Boil the squash in a generous amount of water for 20 minutes. Remove from the water and, once they are cool enough to be handled, cut a lid off the top of each squash and reserve. Scoop out the pips with a spoon, but leave the flesh intact. Turn the squash upside down to drain any excess liquid.

Soak the shiitake mushrooms in boiling water for 30 minutes.

In the meanwhile, heat the oil and butter in a saucepan and braise the onion until translucent and tender. Remove from the pan and set aside. In the same pan, fry the brown mushrooms over a high heat, not filling the pan too much at once, or they will draw water. Brown just slightly.

Drain the soaked shiitake mushrooms, reserving the liquid. Braise them in the pan with the black mushrooms until very light brown. Discard any gritty residue in the pan, then deglaze the pan with the reserved shiitake mushroom liquid.

Still in the same pan combine all the mushrooms, onion, potato and vegetable stock. Cook until the potato is tender and the flavours are well distributed – approximately 15 minutes. Liquidise the soup, but leave it slightly 'lumpy'. Add a few drops of the truffle oil and season with salt and black pepper. Keep hot.

Warm the gem squash in the oven or by steaming them briefly in a saucepan. Fill the squash shells with the mushroom soup and replace their 'lids'.

To serve, place a dollop of mashed potato on each plate and press the filled squash into it, to secure it to the plate. Serves 4 as a starter or light lunch

Ring a Ring o' Rosies

Roses in the courtyard fountain of the Dar Les Cigognes hotel in Marrakech.

My darling aunt Hanna was a bosomy lady. Her hugs were overwhelming. At her bosom one felt safe, cosseted, reassured, loved … and she always smelt of *vieille rose.*

On my father's side of the family, aunty Hester also afforded me some special rose memories. Her green fingers could coax the meanest little slip to flourish and flower within one season. My dad used to buy rose plants in black bags; thereafter his sister would beg a slip to plant. Her mixed garden was unstructured, rather wild and intriguing – a place that naturally lent itself to hunting for fairies under the ferns. Aunty Hester's garden was fragrant with honeysuckle, jasmine, geraniums, carnations, petunias and … roses. I once told her that my mom loved roses, which obliged her to pick a bunch for us to take home! My mom never knew about this, thinking simply that her sister-in-law was kind and generous. Secretly, it was I who loved the roses and I held the almost gaudily coloured bunch under my delighted nose all the way home. Off the record, Mom would have preferred pink, white and salmon only. On that trip I discovered the fragrance of the red rose, the timidity of the soft pink variety and the robustness of the yellow rose.

<hr />

My mom loved her home, keeping it crisp and clean, a few flowers here and there, the smell of baking, and all the touches that make for loving families, such as her recipe for hand lotion with glycerine and rose-water. As a child it never occurred to me that rose-water could be used for anything but lotions, until Mom came across a recipe for Greek butter cookies flavoured with rose-water. We rolled the buttery, nutty dough into little fingers with tapered ends and placed them, crescent-shaped, on the baking tray. The recipe warned that they should be baked through but still pale when they came out of the oven. Once on the cooling rack, we gently sprinkled them with rose-water and the kitchen became a capsule of buttery baking and rose fragrances. Once cool, they were gently packed into a large cookie tin, every layer liberally dusted with icing sugar, and the lid firmly replaced.

Over the next few days we proudly presented these little treasures to our guests with a few pale pink rose petals nestled in-between. Removing the lid was a little problematic in that it was a tight fit, but the pain of my prying fingertips simply evaporated in the rosy fragrance once the lid was off. For a while Mom was not her usual generous self in passing the recipe on to friends. It was as if our success went to our heads! Fortunately this silliness did not last long – it is so much better to share and enjoy together. Today *kourabiedes* may be encountered all over – some better than others, but in my memory, none surpassing Mom's. Butter, apple, almonds, honey and rose-water … an unbeatable combination.

Sweetmeats at Elana Bosini's birthday celebration on Skiathos.

We had the honour of presenting a meal to Sir Elton John, a group of his friends and some promising local artists under his patronage. He most enjoyed the option of helping himself to buffet food, in small quantities, but concentrating on his favourites. Among the guests was a prominent man of Armenian origin and his charming, stylish wife. The dessert offerings included a glass cake stand piled high with cigar-shaped phyllo-pastries filled with rose-flavoured apple, generously buttered and baked. These pale golden sticks were drizzled with honey and sprinkled with toasted almonds. As anticipated, we constantly had to rebuild the stack. The Armenian couple lingered at the buffet table to have another and another. They loved the Middle Eastern flavours. (Sir Elton enjoyed them too!)

As I write, my early summer garden is coming into its own. After some scorched-earth building renovations I managed to save one of the original plants, a scented rose geranium, by planting it temporarily in a black plastic bag. In position in the bare bed, cut back to two short stems, it looked very sad at first. The little tuft of grey santolina alongside and a cluster of pointy, bearded iris leaves looked lonely. Just a few months later, the effects of our home-brew compost, some scatterings of bone meal and regular watering have produced a promising bed of mauve rose geranium flowers, flutters of bearded iris and an undulating carpet of santolina.

Brushing against a rose geranium will be a joy forever. Such a modest plant with such a generous spirit. Originally, I had no idea how to use this herb in the kitchen. At first it was merely part of a decorative arrangement, but it bothered me that I did not use the fragrant leaves. One day I wondered about alternative flavours for custard. A drop of almond essence provided a wonderful flavour profile for little apple tarts. Grated nutmeg, cinnamon and even *elachi* (cardamom) were further tasty changes. On a whim I rinsed a few leaves (from my arrangement!) and popped them into the piping hot custard. Within half an hour the fragrance was fixed. But do remove the wilted leaves before serving. I once used an old puffin jug to serve rose geranium custard, but I must have missed one when fishing out the leaves, which resulted in a rather unattractive, custard-and-limp-leaf emission from the puffin's mouth, into a guest's pudding bowl!

A little Middle Eastern trick is to place a few washed rose geranium leaves at the bottom of a cake tin before pouring in the batter. Once baked, the cake will be subtly flavoured, and, as it is turned out, the leaves can be peeled off the bottom of the cake and discarded.

Rose geranium (above) and the puffin jug (below).

Apple and Rose-water Bâtons

**4 Golden Delicious
apples, peeled, cored
and thinly sliced
45 ml castor sugar
a dash of lemon juice
50–100 ml rose-water
125 g butter
500 g phyllo pastry**

To prepare the filling, place the apple slices in a saucepan with the castor sugar and lemon juice. Poach briefly over a low heat as the apples draw their own juices and the sugar dissolves. It's important that the apples remain crispy. If necessary, scoop out the apples while the sauce reduces to a syrup. Add the rose-water and stir in well.

Preheat the oven to 180 °C. Grease a baking tray.

Melt the butter. Place a sheet of phyllo pastry horizontally on a cutting board. Brush some butter over it before cutting it, top to bottom, into three strips. Spoon some apple filling at the bottom end of each and roll them up, folding in the ends to seal and to keep in the juice. Brush each roll with more butter and place on the baking tray. Continue in the same vein with the phyllo sheets until all the filling is used up. Bake for about 15 minutes. The rolls should be a soft golden colour. Remove from the oven and leave to cool.

Sprinkle liberally with icing sugar and serve immediately with a glass of chilled sweet wine. Makes ±10 bâtons

Rose-water Cordial

**500 g sugar
375 ml water
50 ml lemon juice
red food colouring
50 ml rose-water**

In a saucepan, bring the sugar, water and lemon juice to the boil then simmer until the syrup is thick enough to coat the back of a spoon.

Add some colouring and stir through thoroughly. The amount of colouring depends on your own preference, so add it little by little until the required colour is attained.

Finally, stir in the rose-water. Here again, not all brands of rose-water have the same degree of fragrance, so it will vary. You decide how much you would like, then simmer the mixture briefly.

Pour into clean, dry bottles while piping hot, and seal. To serve, dilute the syrup to taste with cold water and crushed ice. Makes ±500 ml

KOURABIEDES

250 g butter
200 g icing sugar
5 ml vanilla extract
500 ml cake flour
100 g blanched almonds, toasted and
  chopped
15 ml rose-water
icing sugar for dusting

In a mixing bowl, beat the butter, icing sugar and vanilla together until fluffy and creamy. Add the flour and almonds and mix to a smooth dough. Chill in the refrigerator until firm.

Preheat the oven to 160 °C and line a baking tray with non-stick baking paper.

Using about 2 tablespoons (30 ml) at a time, shape the dough into crescents. Place on the baking paper and bake for about 15 minutes. They must not brown.

Leave to cool on a wire rack, sprinkle with the rose-water and dust liberally with icing sugar. Makes ±20

Lemon water at la Petite Tarte.

A fountain in the Jardins Majorelle in Marrakech.

Jack and Jill

An old fishing boat on the lake in Kastoria, Greece.

THAT PAIL OF WATER

Throughout my childhood, on each trip to our holiday house in Kommetjie, just as we got a little beyond Muizenberg, we developed a thirst. Always. Every time. And my father always pulled up at a niche in a stone garden wall where a small but steady stream of crystal clear water flowed from a pipe set in the arch of the niche. Below, it dropped into a clear, clean basin that overflowed into a stormwater drain. Too small to reach the pipe, we would drink from my dad's hands – the sweetest, coolest water imaginable. Dad assured us it was clean. According to the Bible, once water has flowed over seven stones it will be pure. Not to be taken literally today, though!

WATERY PELION

The ferry docked in Volos quite late. En route to the Holy Meteora in central Greece, we had to overnight in Volos. The assistant at the car hire company encouraged us to drive up into the Pelion Mountain to find a hostelry in one of the quaint traditional villages. 'Portaria is close by,' he said, 'and lovely. Try the Xenia Hotel.'

Notwithstanding the righthand-side driving, dozens of hair-pin bends and the pitch black darkness, we reached Portaria's Xenia Hotel soon enough. Lennie and our friend Jane Olive refused to leave the car as the place looked too dreary. I was reticent to drive around one more hair-pin …

'But,' suggested Jane, 'there was a promising sign just a few metres back.' We reversed and saw it: Hotel Despotiko. They forced me to drive up a road so narrow that there was no room to open a car door … and steep … and relentlessly stony and bumpy. At the top was a T-junction and opposite a parking area with a 'No Parking' notice. I parked there.

Jane, determined to find Hotel Despotiko, jumped out and traipsed further up the road. We waited gloomily. Suddenly she reappeared, talking excitedly and gesticulating. After 20 manoeuvres we were back on the road and climbed even higher – all the way in first gear. The next corner necessitated another 20 manoeuvres and the same at the following one. Then, facing downhill, we slowly rolled down and parked in a magical square with a giant plane tree near a crisp, running, marble fountain. With great relief we inhaled the fresh mountain air as the breeze rustled the plane leaves and we listened to the sound of water, water, water, everywhere.

Relaxing, we turned our thoughts to dinner and were directed towards the village. Up along a narrow lane to the town hall and then left, downhill. We passed

Yannis and Maria's daughter, Georgia, drinking from a fountain in the mountains above Skiathos, circa 1994.

a couple from Athens who kindly told us we were heading in the wrong direction and showed us the way. They advised us to go to the tavern on the left of the small lane at the bottom of the hill. It had the edge over the others, they assured us.

We were directed to a table on the sidewalk alongside a fast-flowing furrow of mountain water. Settling in and marking time before the obligatory decisions, we asked our waiter for some mineral water. Wordlessly he turned from us, took a large old earthenware jug from the shelf and in one smooth movement, scooped up water from the stream. He placed the dripping jug on our paper tablecloth saying: 'Is sweet water, good water. Drink!' And we did.

We do recall the food as memorable, simple and good … but it was the water that we will taste and feel forever: crisp, cool, crystal clear and heavenly.

A beautiful old fountain at the Hotel Despotiko in Portaria, Pelion, Greece.

ARAKA

The desert air, the heat and dust made us thirsty. Khaled had taken us to a market on a railway line! It felt as though it was a lifetime away from downtown Cairo and we needed a rest. Yet we forged ahead, fascinated by the variety of goods: bedroom suites in gaudy pastels, exquisite Art Deco light fittings, Art Nouveau vases, toiletries, pure white cottons and ludicrous combinations of colours printed on velours, tiles both antique and new Italian, Mashrabiya screens and old carved woodwork, alabaster incongruities and eventually, what we had been looking for, chandelier crystals. Real, hand-cut, antique, exquisite crystals of all shapes and sizes.

Suddenly a train hooted. Everyone and everything had to move off the railway line … only to be put back again as soon as the train had passed! With my new collection of old crystals we made our way back to the taxis. While at a pavement café we were offered small glasses with our bottled water. The brand of the water was Baraka, meaning 'a gift or blessing'. Our little water glasses were wet with crystal water droplets. The Westerner in me wanted to dry them and polish them, but Khaled explained that a host shows his generosity and hospitality by passing God's precious gift of water on to his guests.

THE UBIQUITOUS LIGHT SUGAR-SYRUP

From time to time one comes across a recipe for a cocktail, a sorbet or a sauce in which to macerate fresh fruit. A light syrup is called for and is something that could be kept in the refrigerator.

Mix equal quantities of water and sugar and heat gently until the sugar dissolves. Bring the syrup to boiling point, then leave to cool down. Bottle and keep chilled.

$\mathcal{P}$OACHED CHICKEN SALAD

This is the recipe that gave me a new regard for this easy, healthy method of preparing chicken breasts. Be sure to buy the best chicken available, as the simplicity of the method will not mask anything dubious in the taste, texture or appearance of the chicken. Everything revolves around simple basics and true flavours.

1–2 heads butter lettuce
1 small bunch flat-leaf parsley
1–2 sticks celery, finely sliced
½ red pepper, diced
6–8 poached chicken breasts (see recipe below)
olive oil for drizzling

DRESSING
250 ml plain yoghurt
15 ml tahini
5 ml honey
30 ml lemon juice
2 ml turmeric

Prepare the dressing by pouring the ingredients into a screw-top bottle large enough to contain it all with space to spare. Close the bottle tightly and shake vigorously to combine. Leave to chill.

Rinse the vegetables well. Remove the outer leaves of the lettuces and cut each heart in quarters. Pull the leaves off the parsley stalks and reserve.

Slice the chicken breasts diagonally into 1-cm slices. Arrange them in a bowl and pour over the dressing. Turn to cover all the pieces well. Spoon the chicken onto a serving platter and surround with the loose lettuce leaves and hearts. Sprinkle the parsley and celery over the leaves and the diced red pepper over the chicken.

Just before serving, drizzle over a little olive oil to make the salad glisten and sparkle. Serves 6 as a light meal

$\mathcal{P}$OACHED CHICKEN BREASTS

6–8 skinless chicken breasts, deboned and rinsed

POACHING LIQUID
750 ml cold water
2 medium carrots, chopped
1 stick celery
1 leek
a few parsley stalks
salt and black pepper

Prepare the poaching liquid well in advance.

In a saucepan, bring the water, vegetables and parsley to the boil, then simmer for approximately 30 minutes. Strain and discard the vegetables and parsley (preferably onto a compost heap).

Add salt and pepper to taste. Leave to cool down altogether. I tend to keep some of this vegetable stock in my refrigerator most of the time, for use as a base for soups, sauces and vegetable juice drinks.

Pour sufficient stock into a saucepan (ultimately to cover the breasts) and bring to the boil. Slide the chicken breasts into the liquid, which will then come off the boil. Keep it on a medium heat until it starts to boil again. Remove the saucepan from the stovetop and leave to stand for 20 minutes. Cut open a breast to test for doneness. The short cooking time should suffice and will avoid the meat toughening. The resulting poached chicken can be used in various ways, although I enjoy using these breasts in the salad above.

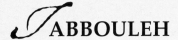ABBOULEH

Soaking burghul wheat – that is as easy as it gets. Not even in hot water …

120 g burghul wheat
200 g finely chopped flat-leaf parsley
75 g finely chopped mint
200 g finely sliced spring onions

DRESSING
juice of 2 lemons
100 ml extra virgin olive oil
salt and black pepper

Place the wheat in a bowl and pour in sufficient cold water to cover it. Leave to soak for 15 minutes.

To make the dressing, combine the lemon juice, olive oil and salt and pepper to taste.

Drain the wheat and squeeze out as much water as possible. Pour the dressing over, then add the parsley, mint and spring onions. Mix thoroughly. When tasting the salad, the lemony sharpness should be distinct. This salad may be chilled but benefits from returning to room temperature before serving.

Serve the salad with the pale green leaves of cos lettuce hearts, to be used as little scoops. Serves 4 as a starter

GOOD IDEAS …

Long, hot summer days require tall glass jugs of cool water ready to cool one down … flavoured water reverts to its original meaning with slices of lime, lemon, strawberry or cucumber and leaves of mint, lemon grass, Vietnamese basil or mixed herbs.

Prevent greens from turning grey by poaching green beans, spinach, peas and lettuce briefly in a little boiling water in a pot without a lid. Cool them immediately by rinsing under cold running water.

inocybe
euthules

Amanita muscaria

Under a Toadstool Crept a Wee Elf

Amanita pantherina

Volvaria speciosa

inocybe hirtella

Toadstools are romantic props in fairy-tale illustrations. Mushrooms are food. As a child I found this difficult to comprehend. I just love fairies jumping over toadstools, crowned frogs sitting on them and elves sitting in their shade. And of all their colours, I like the red toadstools with white spots best.

I remember driving past a fairy sanctuary in Swellendam once and thought it should be inspected to see if there were toadstools (or perhaps a few giant mushrooms to harvest).

What a beautiful town Swellendam is. My parents lived there some time back – but only for two short years. Yet they loved the area for its beauty, the kind folk and the abundance of produce. Dad, an inspector of schools, never came home without some or other produce-gift: dried peaches, farm butter, *beskuit* (rusks), tomato seedlings, *boerpampoen* (a large pumpkin), lemon syrup … but never mushrooms.

Lennie and I stopped in Swellendam a few years ago. Looking for a suitable lunch venue, we were directed to a lovely old building opposite the Drostdy. There were mostly large tables to share and a terse menu that stated 'Today's Menu: Take It or Leave It!' Taking the bull by the horns, Lennie said that he was not a meat eater and was there something available for him. 'Oh absolutely,' answered the Proprietress, 'my husband went mushroom picking in the mountains this morning and you'll have wild mushrooms.'

We could hardly believe the generosity. My platter of meat and vegetables could have fed an army. There was even a portion of boiled beef with its own vegetables. Not exactly regular restaurant fare, but I enjoyed it all the more for that reason. Imagine tender beef with carrots, turnips and potatoes, all with flavours intermingling. The little wait, once I had been served, had Lennie slightly nervous. 'Take It or Leave It' was both amusing and ominous. Then his order arrived – the most beautiful, fresh, wild mountain mushrooms, prepared with butter, herbs and garlic, presented on a serving platter from which one served oneself. As it became obvious that 'my' vegetables were also 'our' vegetables (except for the 'beefy' ones), I took the liberty of having some mushrooms as well … This unexpectedly lavish, yet unpretentious meal, revealed the abundance of the Swellendam valley. When living there all those years ago, I would never have thought to look for mushrooms under the oaks.

Our dearly beloved Ridgeback, Camille, sunning herself in the garden.

By all accounts Camille was a Ridgeback, but she had inherited her mother's slimness, finely cut head and a few stray, soft-blonde Afghan hairs sprouting from her tummy. However, her father's genes proved to be strong. She was a beautiful colour – golden brown with a rather dark muzzle, eyes and ears. Her bark was intimidating and made one feel safe to be with her. She loved her walks. On a beautiful autumn day, after the previous day's rain, we went mushroom picking in the Cecilia Forest near Kirstenbosch on the slopes of Table Mountain. As a novice, I was rather careful. Armed with an array of handbooks and field guides on edible and poisonous South African fungi, we set off. Baskets would have looked more elegant, but with Camille on a leash I thought that plastic bags would be more practical. We had an enjoyable walk and found quite a few ceps and pine rings. There were others too, but not knowing enough, I left them.

UNDER A TOADSTOOL CREPT A WEE ELF

Once home, I called on the expertise of our friend Lina to identify my harvest. Without hesitation I was invited over. Eugene, Lina's son, then still at school, was also there. And stretched across the kitchen, just above one's head, were many strings of drying mushrooms, evidence of Eugene's pickings on Table Mountain. From early childhood Lina's children had been educated to respect, nurture, enjoy and harvest nature. The family also cooks delicious food, prepared simply, yet emphasising basic flavours.

Our mushroom meal that evening was memorable for the abundance, flavours and novelty. Doubting Thomas Len nervously tasted some buttery, garlicky mushrooms – and then could not contain himself. If we felt a little under the weather that night, it had nothing to do with the wrong mushrooms and everything to do with over-indulgence!

Dried mushrooms usually have a most tantalising fragrance, so concentrated that they can enhance a dish of fresh mushrooms with a taste akin to truffles. When rehydrating dried mushrooms in water, I usually include that water in the subsequent recipe. If doing this, take care to discard any sandy residues which may have formed.

Say 'mushrooms', and Lennie will answer 'on toast!' Is that not one of *the* ultimate in retro treats? We are from such diverse backgrounds, yet there are so many points on which we agree and where our cultures meet. Mushrooms on toast is one such point. Marmite™ toast fingers for ailing children is another, as is a piece of burnt toast scraped away not being a disaster. Yet another is the perfect marriage of toast and marmalade.

Two things I love, and Lennie does not, are squashed sardines on toast with a squeeze of lemon, and anchovy toast with lots of pepper. We do agree, though, that retro or not, they remain legitimate. But toast and mushrooms was supper fare in both households. Lennie claims that mushrooms didn't have names in those days, but thinking back they were the white, button variety. Both mothers, mindful of their families' well-being, washed the mushrooms, after which they were chopped and stewed in butter. Daring changes included starting the 'stew' by braising some onions first, then adding mushrooms, or to finish the dish off by adding milk. Budget allowing, diced bacon bits were added.

Robert Carrier elevates 'mushrooms on toast' to 'Swiss bacon and mushroom toasts'. For 'Swiss' read cholesterol-laden … and delicious! He prescribes crustless sandwiches made with thinly sliced mushrooms, rindless bacon, and grated Gruyère cheese and thick cream. The sandwiches are then dipped in beaten egg and pan-fried in butter! According to Carrier: 'Lay a knife and fork to eat the sandwich as a first course, or cut them into bite-size pieces before passing them around with drinks.'

Today we do not wash our mushrooms. We can be picky about the type, and we do not stew them, but the combinations we enjoyed then are still appropriate. I have tried to understand Shirley Conran's 'Life is too short to stuff a mushroom', but … they are just sooo good. I wonder if she had a good, quick recipe and the proper mushrooms?

A handful of breadcrumbs, chopped parsley, grated Parmesan, a daring bit of crushed garlic, a drop of olive oil or a knob of butter, all mixed together, spread into a mushroom 'cup' and grilled in the oven. So easy, so quick and what a difference to our short lives!

Our friend and inspiration, Lina de Villiers (top), and (bottom) her son and daughter-in-law, Eugene and Elana Bosini.

CHAMPIGNONS À LA GRECQUE

Various vegetables such as celery, fennel, courgettes, onions and leeks are prepared à la Grecque *by the French. Somehow, in spite of the name, this does not seem to be usual in Greece.*

250 g really small button mushrooms, wiped clean
45 ml olive oil
45 ml water
juice of ½ lemon, or to taste
2 tomatoes, skinned and chopped
4 peppercorns, lightly pounded
6 coriander seeds, lightly pounded
1 sprig of thyme
salt and black pepper to taste

With the exception of the mushrooms, combine all the ingredients in a saucepan and bring to the boil. Allow to cool for approximately 5 minutes before adding the mushrooms, then simmer very gently for a further 5 minutes.

Remove the mushrooms with a slotted spoon and continue to boil the sauce until it reduces to a thicker concentrate. Pour the sauce over the mushrooms, then leave to macerate.

Serve at room temperature with crusty bread. Serves 4 as a starter

UNDER A TOADSTOOL CREPT A WEE ELF

$\mathcal{M}$ USHROOM RISOTTO

A comfort food that is always appropriate, this risotto is a lifesaver when we have 'nothing in the fridge'. I wouldn't like to guess how frequently risottos have saved my reputation. And vegetable stock is so easy to make that I afford myself no excuse!

1.5 litres water	500 g brown mushrooms, wiped
2 carrots, chopped	and chopped
2 sticks celery, chopped	a knob of butter
1 fat leek, topped and tailed	olive oil
a few stalks of parsley	375 ml risotto rice
salt	125 ml dry white wine
1 medium onion, finely chopped	200 ml grated Parmesan or
butter or olive oil for braising	pecorino cheese
15 ml butter	an extra knob of butter
15 ml sunflower oil	

Pour the water into a saucepan, add the carrots, celery, leek and parsley, and boil for approximately 30 minutes. Add salt to taste. Strain, discarding the vegetables, but keep the stock on the boil.

In a pan, braise the chopped onion in some butter or olive oil until it is soft and golden, but not brown. Keep warm.

In a frying pan, heat a tablespoon (15 ml) each of butter and sunflower oil, then fry the mushrooms over a moderately high heat. The mushrooms should not be crowded in the pan or they will draw water and stew; not a good idea if you want to retain the essential mushroom flavour. Keep warm.

In a large saucepan, heat a knob of butter and a little olive oil. Add the rice to the butter-oil and stir to coat the grains and to heat them thoroughly. Add a cup (250 ml) of the boiling stock – be careful with the steam that will be generated – and boil at a medium heat. Once this stock has been absorbed, add another half cup (125 ml) of stock. Cook gently until that too is absorbed. Repeat, stirring regularly until all the stock has been used up. Pour in the wine and continue to cook until absorbed. This process will take 20–25 minutes. By this stage, the rice should be *al dente* and creamy at the same time. Should the rice need more liquid, add a little boiling water. Finally, off the heat, stir in the onions, mushrooms, cheese and the extra knob of butter. Serve immediately.

If you like, you can vary the dish with the addition of garlic, sprigs of thyme, crispy bacon or a few drops of truffle oil. Serves 4 as a main course

The front and back of the business card
of a confectioner's in Psiri, Athens.

Όλα βουτηγμένα στο δερμπέτι.

Τα γλυκά μας δίδονται και σε πακέτο

ΤΑ ΣΕΡΜΠΕΤΙΑ στου ψυρρή

Αισχύλου 3 Τηλ.:3245.862 - Πλατεία Ψυρρή

Το ονομάσαμε <<Σερμπέτια>> από την λέξη cerbet που σημαίνει σιρόπι, είδος αρωματικού ποτού και μεταφορικά τα ερωτικά γλυκόλογα και φιλιά.

Η αυλή του <<σπιτιού>> μας, μυρίζει κανέλλα και ζάχαρη και συνεχίζει να σερβίρει, *καφέ με λουκουμάκι*, **το γλυκό της αγάπης** βουτηγμένο σε πλούσια σοκολάτα γάλακτος και πολλές, πολλές ξεχωριστές γεύσεις.

Δοκιμάστε το υπέροχο **καζάν ντιπί**, τις *φωλιές σοκολάτα*, το <<**σαρίκι**>> με την κρέμα πασπαλισμένο με μπόλικη άχνη και κανέλλα, αλλά και *μυρωδάτο γαλακτομπούρεκο*, ξεροψημένο *μπακλαβά* με καρύδι και αμύγδαλο, **κιουνεφέ κρέμα**, καθώς επίσης το εκμέκ πολίτικο, το *γκιουζέλ σοκολάτα* και *πορτοκάλι*, την περίφημη **ροδακινόπιτά μας**. Ακόμα μπορείτε να απολαύσετε *γιαούρτι με μέλι* με καταπληκτικούς συνδυασμούς γλυκών του κουταλιού... Καφέδες όλοι, ανάλογα με τη διάθεση σας, από τον *κλασσικό ελληνικό*, μέχρι espresso, cappuccino, *γαλλικό, σοκολάτα ρόφημα*, και τσάι σε πολλά αρώματα, ...και το μοναδικό **ρακόμελο της πόλης** σε καραφάκι ή μπρίκι... η επιλογή δική σας

Eating Her Curds and Whey

I was a child of the 'Flats', as much of my childhood was spent in Ottery and Retreat on the Cape Flats. But how different it was from today.

At school my friends included Rudolf Bokelman, Ralph Rix, Rita Schaap and another Rudolf – Rudolf Buhr – all children of the German settlers who tamed the sandy soil of Philippi, Ottery, Lansdowne and Retreat through hard work, perseverance and by being in tune with nature. The area used to be the vegetable basket of the Cape.

In addition to growing vegetables, these farmers were totally self-sufficient with regard to poultry, pork, eggs, dairy, and even fruit and flowers. One of our most joyful outings was the bazaar on the first Saturday of May every year at the German church in Philippi. My joy had everything to do with the food. The tables were piled high with homemade pork products such as smoked sausages, bacon, tee-wurst and met-wurst. Other tables offered fresh vegetables, fruit, flowers and eggs, freshly churned farm butter, bottles of quark, cream cheese and yoghurt. There was a table with lemon syrup and ginger beer, a pancake corner, biscuits and cakes. Two cakes that I adored were *Butterkuchen* and the German cheesecake.

I was five when I first encountered the perplexing phenomenon of 'cheese cake' when Mom took me to visit Aunt Hentie. The wife of a German farmer, she was a diligent housewife who worked alongside her husband to support the family. Yet she also found time to alter clothing for my mother. These Germans were inherently hospitable and she was no exception. No sooner were we welcomed than we could smell the coffee brewing. The home always smelled faintly of baking – and my mind raced: cake, cookies, pies … what delight was in store? Well, it was German coffee in one of those pots with a lid, part of which one had to push down slowly. There was farm milk and there was a cup for me!

The cake was one I had never seen before, ever. It looked like a tart with a high crust, filled to the brim. Aunt Hentie kindly asked whether we would like some cheesecake. That sent my mind racing. The only cheeses I knew were Cheddar and Gouda and I really could not face a sweet cake made with either of these. Mom was most impressed with this family recipe. I noticed that the cake was dotted with currants, which appealed to me. All the same, I said 'no-thank-you' as properly as I could and fell into a bit of a decline.

Time came for Mom and Aunt Hentie to discuss and try on the altered clothing. Left alone and really puzzled, I took my mother's plate and stole the tiniest sliver of cheesecake, gouging an extra currant from the cake.

When they returned I asked if I could please have a little slice of cake … I've never looked back!

Everyone knows the urban legend of the lady who attended a society dinner at a five-star hotel and was so impressed by the delicious dessert that she sent a note to the kitchen requesting the recipe. She was presented with the treasure. But with it was an invoice for many hundreds of dollars, which she bravely paid in order to save face. My mother maintained that it was our carrot cake recipe, which she had received as a chain-letter posted world-wide by the insulted woman in protest against the chef's nastiness.

My mother's recipe is a simpler version of the one Lennie bakes at la Petite Tarte. Some people may not care for the pineapple, in which case Mom's would be more appropriate. However, both versions require a sumptuous topping, and that is the cheese connection in this story. Sugar, butter, vanilla extract and cream cheese, that's all it is – but addictive, of course.

Our dear friend Karen passed a recipe on to us that sounded absolutely ambrosial, and, I thought, rather like Liz's carrot cake, which we enjoyed one memorable evening. Roger had invited us over for eight one evening. Dinner, we concluded. Looking forward to the evening, Lennie thought it would be diplomatic to warn our hostess that he does not eat red meat.

She shrieked with laughter: 'Red meat, my darling … you'd hardly get any of that with your coffee and cake!'

In due course we discovered that they enjoyed early suppers and coffee and cake afterwards, at about eight. Liz's carrot cake was absolutely delicious: moist, flavoured with cinnamon, walnuts, coconut and pineapple and topped with an extraordinary sweet-tart fluffiness. We really did not miss the red meat at all!

Our coffee shop and salon du thé, la Petite Tarte in Cape Town (opposite), and my mom's original handwritten carrot cake recipe (right).

Julle was pas weg toe onthou ek die van die koekresep wat jy wou gehad het & hier volg dit.

Carrot Cake

1 cup sugar
1 " oil   } Beat well
3 eggs
1½ cups sugar flour
1½ teasp. B. Powder.   } Sift together & add to egg mixture.
1½ " " Bic of soda
2 " " Cinnamon
2 cups coarsely grated Carrots   } Add carrots & nuts. Stir well. Pour into 2 layer cake pans & bake at 350° for ± ½ hour
1 cup nuts.

Icing : 1½ cups icing sugar 1 Tablesp. butter & smooth cream cheese. (± Tablesp.)

Johnny baie baie dankie vir jou & Len vir die afdankie, kamer lyk al klaar baie beter. So bly jy het die ou lekke ou lampkap hier weg, hier is so baie dinge in die huis wat hinder lik is & dan weer ander dinge wat ek nodig het wat ek maar gedurig in aan te koy. dit hinder ook. Dit was so lekke bic a heerlike Lufie.

HE CARROT CAKE
legally adopted by la Petite Tarte

500 ml granulated sugar
4 large eggs
3 ml vanilla extract
375 ml vegetable oil
500 ml cake flour
5 ml baking powder
10 ml bicarbonate of soda
10 ml ground cinnamon
5 ml salt
750 ml grated carrots (we use a little more)
200 ml desiccated coconut
250 ml chopped walnuts (or ½ walnuts and ½ pecan nuts)
250 ml drained crushed pineapple (but not over-drained!)

TOPPING
125 g butter, slightly softened
500 g icing sugar, sifted
250 g cream cheese
5 ml vanilla extract
chopped walnuts for sprinkling

Preheat the oven to 180 °C. Grease and line 2 x 23-cm cake tins with baking paper.

Beat the sugar, eggs and vanilla extract together, gradually mixing in the oil. Sift together the flour, baking powder, bicarbonate of soda, cinnamon and salt, then mix into the egg mixture. Combine the grated carrots, coconut, walnuts and pineapple, then add to the batter. Pour into the prepared cake tins and bake for approximately 1 hour.

For the topping, cream the butter in the bowl of a food mixer and gradually add about half the icing sugar. Beat until fluffy. Add the cream cheese, then beat on slow speed. Finally, add the rest of the icing sugar and the vanilla extract. Stop beating as soon as it is all mixed in, otherwise the topping will become too runny.

Turn the cakes out onto cooling racks and peel off the baking paper.

Spread one cake with half of the icing mixture. Place the other cake on top and spread the rest of the topping over the top of it. Sprinkle generously with chopped walnuts.

EATING HER CURDS AND WHEY

$\mathscr{S}$MOKED SALMON TROUT PÂTÉ

Cream cheese is also frequently used as a base for savoury dishes. A favourite of mine is this smoked salmon trout pâté, based on a recipe of Ina Paarman's. It makes a wonderful starter.

300 g smoked salmon trout, chopped
250 g cream cheese
125 ml fresh cream
15 ml lemon juice
50 g fresh dill, chopped
a pinch of cayenne pepper
crème fraîche to garnish
salmon trout caviar (traviar) to garnish
melba toast for serving

Blend the salmon trout, cream cheese, fresh cream, lemon juice, dill and cayenne pepper together in a blender, stopping from time to time to stir.

Spoon into a single dish or a number of small, individual dishes. Garnish the single, large dish or each of the small dishes with a dollop of crème fraîche and some salmon trout caviar. Serve with fingers of thinly sliced melba toast. Serves 6 as a starter

CREAM CHEESE CAKE

BASE
375 ml crushed Marie biscuits
45 ml melted butter

FILLING
4 eggs
250 ml sugar
5 ml vanilla essence
4 x 250 g tubs cream cheese

TOPPING
125 g sour cream
8 ml sugar
3 ml vanilla essence
mixed berry compote for drizzling

Preheat the oven to 180 °C.

To make the base, mix together the biscuits and butter, then press into a 23-cm springform cake tin.

Beat the eggs and sugar together. Stir in the vanilla essence, then mix in the cream cheese, 1 tub at a time. Pour the mixture into the base and bake for 35 minutes (test after 30 minutes to check if the filling has set). Leave to cool.

Mix together the topping ingredients, then spread over the cooled filling. Return the cheesecake to the oven for another 5 minutes at 180 °C.

To serve, drizzle some berry compote over each slice.

Sheet music, a gift from Mr Kühn (above), and (left) my mother, May de Villiers, and a friend Aunty Cillie, in Adderley Street, dressed for afternoon tea, circa 1950.

Sugar and Spice

The spice markets in Istanbul and Marrakech.

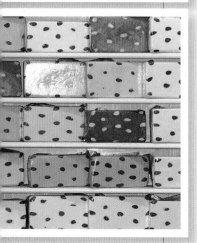

'Teaspoon sweets' sold on the roadside in Cyprus (top), a delicious dessert at Agnantio Restaurant on Skiathos (centre), and nougat in Marrakech, Morocco (bottom).

We were driving through Larnaca in Cyprus, eastwards towards Fig Tree Bay, passing Agia Napa and a few small settlements, when food came to mind. Of all the places we could have chosen, we stopped at a petrol station shop. I don't remember, but I don't think we actually needed petrol.

A quick scan of the shelves revealed only one thing: popular, modern pre-packed offerings. Nonetheless, Lennie's trained eyes spotted some sweet cookies, which looked a little out of place and intriguing enough for us to buy the bigger pack. We drove off sipping fruit juices and tasting the spoils. Those little butter-and-honey-and-nuts-and-seeds-and-sugar-and-spice-and-all-things-nice goodies were unbelievably good. At the time we could not read Greek very well and kept the wrapper, hoping to find more. We were hailing Cyprus as the ultimate country for sweetmeats and sugary confections. Later, when our friends read the wrapper we discovered that these delectable treasures came from Beirut. Shucks, the Lebanese have the edge …

❧

An Egyptian friend took us to Kuweider in Zamalek, Cairo. If my memory serves me right, it is close to the intersection of 26th of July Street and Mansour Mohammed. This is a space dedicated to the sweet tooth. One section dispenses ice creams in flavours quite foreign to us. The rest of the shop stocks cakes of all shapes, sizes and flavours. But it is the honey, phyllo, *kadaifi* (Greek/Turkish pastry with sweetened nuts and saturated in syrup), butter, nuts, spices and syrup sweetmeats that fascinates us.

These tiny (2 x 2 cm) offerings fill huge circular trays 80–100 cm in diameter and are a mass of golden, syrupy texture, sometimes dotted with pistachio nuts, sesame seeds, walnuts or almonds. We ordered large round boxes covered in 'gold leaf' to be filled with these morsels. What an astounding performance! Deft hands (of mostly young men who love showing off) lined the boxes with a very particular type of greaseproof paper before rapidly packing a variety of cookies – in patterns – into the boxes, interspersing the layers with more greaseproof paper. Once full, the paper protruding above the completed layer is folded over and another sheet is placed on top. In a final, theatrical display, the entire contents, keeping its shape in the paper wrapping, is shaken from the box to lie on the hand, then magically turned over and replaced in the box, now upside down. The lid was replaced, a ribbon tied around the box and we had a gift fit for a king! Originally, we were informed, Kuweider was a Lebanese concern.

❧

The sugar and spice quarter of the Khan el Khalili market in Cairo has it all: stall upon stall of spices, sugars, sweets, preserves and many things we did not even know. Everything is displayed in vast quantities: mounds of cloves, star anise, nutmeg, cinnamon, palm sugar tablets, cubed sugar, candy-coloured crystal sugar, pomegranate syrup, sour cherry and vanilla syrup … all of which is mind boggling and totally confusing.

That is what little girls are made of … !

In the name of progress, Cape Town lost so many characterful businesses and their architecturally interesting buildings. One such, on the corner of Adderley and Darling streets, was Fletcher & Cartwright's, a department store with beautiful interiors, refined merchandise and genteel service. Besides clothing and homeware departments, there was a music department with an extensive stock of sheet music, instruments and a most knowledgeable staff. Mr Kuhn, a very tall, slim man with the kindest smile and voice, was my greatest friend. He composed a lullaby and sold copies in the store. He also played the beautiful black piano in the store and encouraged me to sing the lullaby with him.

After the music section, I loved the tearoom most of all. A gentleman would guide us to a table where a waitress in a starched, lace-trimmed apron stood in attendance with the menu. Mom would place her clutch-bag and gloves on a little shelf under the tabletop. I never had any doubt about my choice for tea: the tiered cake stand. Little silver teapots, hot water pots, cups with the F&C monogram, cake plates, napkins and cake forks were soon placed on the table. In the middle there remained a space. My eyes followed the waitress as she collected the tiered stand from the cake counter and brought it to our table. It was like a beautiful, precious crown on our table. Nestled in fluted white paper cases were cream horns, éclairs, meringues, iced chocolate slices, custard slices, *petit fours* and other wondrous things, all of which filled me with desire. But I was allowed only one, and I always, *always*, had a custard slice and always loved it. And made a thorough mess! The waitress, clearing our table, would count the empty paper cases and add them to our bill. Now, is that not civilised?

P.S. If Fletcher & Cartwright were still around and I still a child, I would have warned everyone that the meringues were not gooey inside, the cream horns were full of not-sweet-enough cream that squirted onto one's shirt, and the *petit fours* had almond paste inside!

Although I am not so fond of custard slices any longer, I retain a penchant for layered sweet things: pancakes with a sweet lemon cream, biscuit layers with rich chocolate filling, layers of vanilla butter sponge filled with banana and hazelnut. The recipe that follows is a simple but attractive and delicious variation on the sugar and spice layers.

Rose-water cupcakes at la Petite Tarte.

CARAMELISED PEAR
and phyllo pastries

500 g phyllo pastry
100 g butter, melted
100 g light brown sugar

PEAR FILLING
4 firm but ripe pears
a squeeze of lemon juice
30 ml butter
30 ml white sugar

TO SERVE
clotted cream (if you can find it!) or crème fraîche
nutmeg, cinnamon and/or allspice
icing sugar (optional)

Preheat the oven to 180 °C. Open the phyllo pastry, but keep it covered with a slightly moist cloth while working with the individual sheets. The aim is to prevent the phyllo from drying out.

Spread a sheet of phyllo with melted butter and sprinkle lightly with the sugar. Cover with another sheet of pastry and repeat the butter and sugar process. Cut the two (layered) sheets into squares of approximately 8 cm. Arrange them on a baking tray.

Allow 3–4 of these layered squares per serving. Bake in the oven until barely golden. Take care because they can darken very suddenly. These may be prepared well in advance.

Peel, core and cut the pears into slivers. Squeeze a little lemon juice over the pears to prevent them from discolouring. Melt the butter in a saucepan and add the sugar. Watch carefully as the sugar caramelises to a golden colour. Add the pear pieces and stir gently. The pears will draw water and a syrup will form. Cook briefly but keep the pears crisp. Leave to cool to room temperature.

To serve, place a square of phyllo on a plate and top it with some of the pears. Place a second square over the pears and spoon more pears onto that. Cover with a third square. Add the inevitable dollop of cream or crème fraîche and, finally, sprinkle with a little grated nutmeg, cinnamon or allspice. If you like, dust with some icing sugar. Serves 6

APRICOT AND GINGER BISCUITS

175 g butter
750 ml brown sugar
3 eggs
1 kg cake flour
10 ml ground ginger
5 ml ground cinnamon
20 ml bicarbonate of soda
10 ml baking powder
3 ml salt
125 ml apricot jam
15 ml golden syrup
45 ml brandy
ginger preserve to garnish

Preheat the oven to 180 °C. Grease a baking tray.

Cream the butter and sugar together until pale and light in texture. Mix in the eggs, one at a time.

Sift the flour, ginger, cinnamon, bicarbonate of soda, baking powder and salt together. Mix into the creamed butter mixture. Stir in the apricot jam, golden syrup and brandy.

Scoop out and roll walnut-sized balls of dough. Arrange them on the baking tray and flatten slightly. Leave ample space in between the biscuits.

Bake for about 15 minutes until golden. Add a slice of ginger preserve to the centre of each biscuit. Makes ±24 biscuits

Appelkoosgemmerkoekies.

4 lb meel
3 " geelsuiker } Room
1 " Botter }
½ " varkvet
6 eiers
1E gemmer
1E kaneel
2 pk koeksoda
4 E.B Poeier
1 E. Sout
1t Sout
1Kp appelkooskonfyt
2E goue stroop
¼ kp Brandewyn.
Roer al die bestandele in room mengsel.
Bak lekker!

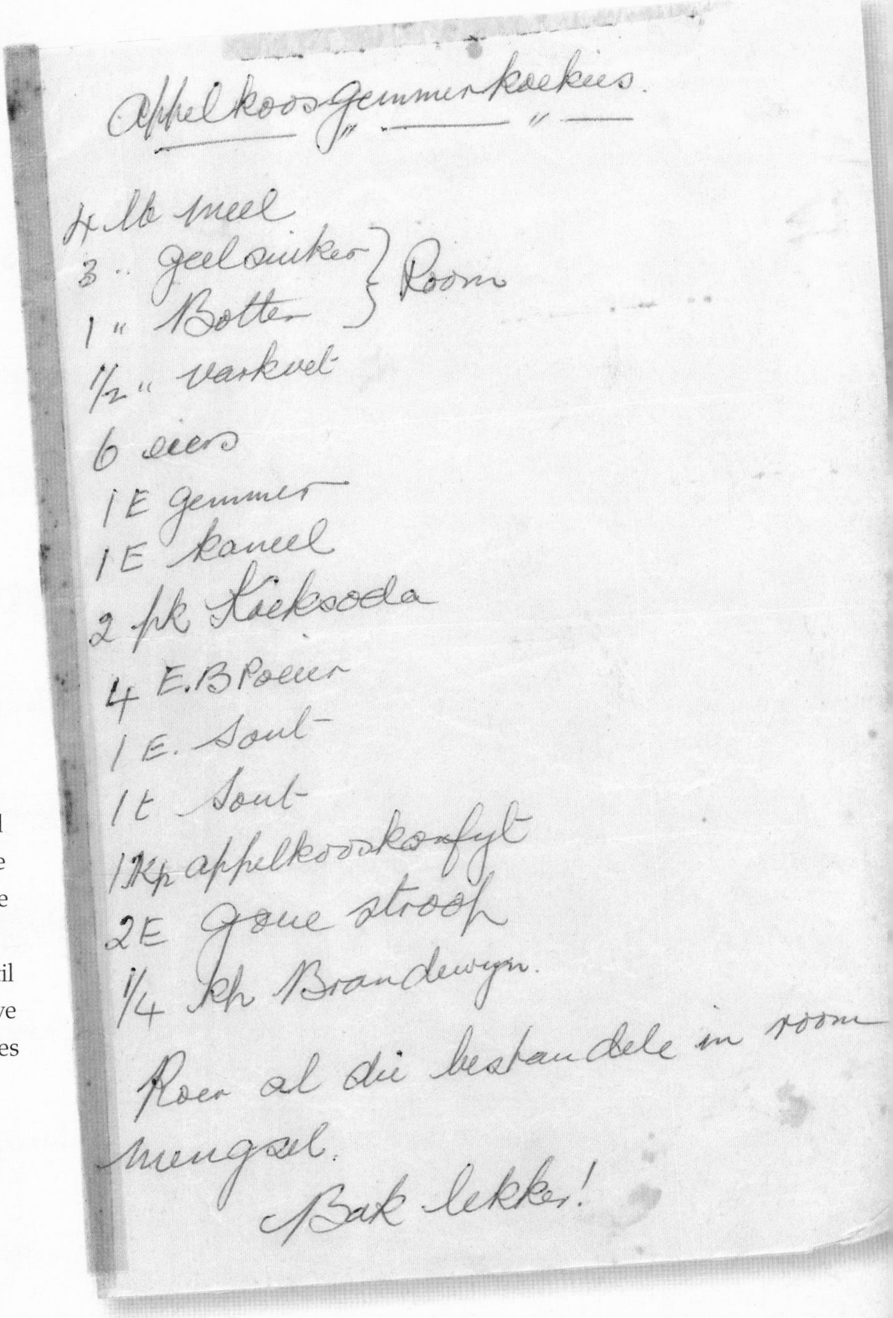

Lalaria beach, Skiathos.

1, 2, 3, 4, 5
Once I Caught
a Fish Alive

*The fish market in Büyükada, Princes'
Islands, Turkey (left), and (right) lunch of
marides (sardines) at Kastro, Skiathos.*

The lovely Annette de Villiers (top) in her beautiful apartment in Paris, and (centre and bottom) fishy encounters at Zigi in Cyprus.

For us, a visit to Paris is not perfect unless our darling friend Annette is there to look after us. Like babies, we spoil easily and Annette loves hosting, treating and spoiling … and seeing our astounded faces. The lovely man in her life, Francois, is as generous and kind as Annette, which is how we landed up at a superb Parisian seafood restaurant one evening. For us fresh fish with an ambrosial, enigmatic, reduced and enriched French sauce is an adventure. For them it is much, much more.

The anguish of an all-French menu turned into relief when they offered to order for us. A lovely bottle of wine helped us to relax. The floodgates opened! Plates, huge napkins, knives and forks and instruments of torture with points and hooks, bowls of intriguing sauces, crisper than crisp salads and fragrant rice arrived. We were both delighted and over-awed. The *pièce de résistance* was a towering structure of lobsters, shellfish, mussels, cockles, oysters, periwinkles and sea urchins. It was a work of art and, intimidated, I felt like retreating into my own shell. But Annette and Francois led the way and introduced us to one sea creature after the other. The implements made sense as we prized periwinkles from their shells and pried into crevices and hidden carapace corners to release the tastiest morsels. The sauces were intended for specific bites, the rice complemented others and the salads were a sophisticated contrast to the seafood.

It was a night of many tastes, surprises and the odd disappointment, of fun and fear, of learning and overcoming prejudice, of bravery (on our part) and finally of total delight as we realised that Francois had settled the bill! Notwithstanding this, our seafood eating habits have remained somewhat staid; we love simplicity too much.

*T*WO FISHY ENCOUNTERS ON CYPRUS

Small as it may be, Cyprus offers a confusing array of weather conditions – all at once and on various parts of the island. On the coast one can bask in the sun while 30 minutes away, up in the Troulos Mountains, thick mists and rain may be prevalent.

Various friends told us about a seaside village where the best fish is served. We left the highway and drove along a less-than-minor road towards the coast. The tiny village sported a number of restaurants at the water's edge. As the only people at the restaurant we selected a table at the waterside. When we announced that we'd come to sample some fish we got a 'what else?' kind of look and were whisked off to the refrigerators to view the possibilities. How frightening! Long fish, short fish, titchy fish, round fish, pale fish, coloured fish …

The trick with Cypriot restaurateurs, we discovered, is to allow them to perplex, confuse and eventually to delight one with their fare. So, we expressed amazement, but remained undecided and were then told which fish was to be ours! The chef set to grilling it. It was so relaxing and the wine so agreeable that we were surprised when the meal appeared. Our whole grilled fish, fragrant with butter, oil and herbs arrived on a large platter. We were quite prepared to serve ourselves and cope with the bones, head, tail and fins in-between, when our chef took out a flat palette-like knife. Deftly he ran the knife along the central bone, lifted the sides off and placed them on a new, hot platter. He neatly removed the head, tail and all the other bones and lay the solid, boneless meat on the second platter.

With that we had olives, extra oily-lemony-herby sauce, green leaf salad and bread. It was an unforgettable meal: two kings sitting at the seaside on a beautiful day, served a simple, honest meal by a nonchalant but kind chef. And nearby a large ginger cat sat watching … and waiting!

A few days later we drove from the sunny coast to the mountains where misty, rainy weather had settled in. Tall trees dripped onto fairy-tale wooden houses. We climbed ever higher and, skirting a little valley, looked down upon a tavern from where a column of smoke was rising, dancing up, up, up. Music and voices drifted up, muted in the soggy weather, but jolly nonetheless. A narrow dirt road turned off unexpectedly and we wound down to the tavern. We were warmly welcomed, taken to a table and offered some wine – either village wine in plain glass bottles of varying shapes and sizes, or real wine with labels and seals. As we were in the mountains, we opted for the village wine. After about ten sips we were quite used to it and after that we started to enjoy it.

It became evident that the large table next to us was actually the tavern family table. *Papous* (grandfathers), *yia-yias* (grandmothers), uncles, aunts, mothers and fathers with children. All jolly, relaxed and all talking at once. We ordered salmon, caught in the local streams. From the family table we had a constant flow of 'Taste this' … little bowls of feta, olives, *tarama* (carp roe), *horta* (green vegetables), *marithes* (small fish) … whatever they thought the foreigners would enjoy.

When our salmon arrived we were delighted that they were *bleu* (lightly poached), done to perfection, succulent and beautifully pink inside. For the moment we were drawn right into the family circle and regaled with kindness and generosity. The village wine had also drawn us into some sort of circle because my head was spinning. Even so, we spent an afternoon in an enchanted environment in the pine forested mountains, hospitably entertained by a local family. Does it get any better?

While working at the beautiful La Residence in Franschhoek, I endeavoured to use products from the environment. The Three Streams Trout and Salmon farm supplied us with thinly sliced smoked salmon trout, sides of smoked salmon, Norwegian smoked salmon and traviar (salmon trout 'caviar'). A great aspect of its products is that they need minimal cooking or interference, as is obvious in the following recipe.

Skopelos Island, Greece (top and bottom), and boating on Skiathos (centre).

LIGHTLY SMOKED FILLETS
of salmon trout with a celeriac salad and pink grapefruit segments

2 lightly smoked fillets of salmon trout
salt and freshly ground black pepper
black onion seeds for sprinkling
watercress to garnish

CELERIAC SALAD AND PINK GRAPEFRUIT
500 g celeriac root, peeled
lemon juice to moisten the celeriac
125 ml good-quality mayonnaise
3–4 Peppadews®, finely diced
2 pink grapefruit

First prepare the salad. Either grate the celeriac root on a medium-coarse grater or use a mandoline vegetable slicer to create thin matchsticks. Place in a bowl and add sufficient lemon juice to moisten the celeriac. Stir in the mayonnaise and diced peppadews.

To prepare the grapefruit, peel them deep enough to remove the membranes of the segments. Cut lengthways into the fruit, just next to a segment membrane, then cut along the other side of the segment, releasing the wedge. Continue all the way around and squeeze out any juice from the empty membranes, reserving it for later use.

The salmon trout fillets are usually generous enough for 2 portions. Cut each fillet in half and season with salt and pepper to taste, then sprinkle with the black onion seeds.

Warm a ridged grill pan until it is smoking hot. Place the fish skin-side down in the pan and cook for 3–4 minutes. Turn and cook for another 4 minutes. Because the fish has been lightly smoked, it should not be over-cooked or it will lose its flavour.

Arrange the fish slices on plates with a little mound of celeriac salad, pink grapefruit segments that have been drizzled with their own juice, and garnished with a tuft of watercress. Serves 4 as a main course

CORIANDER, LIME AND CHILLI PRAWNS

16 large prawns, deveined and heads removed but tails left on
8 kebab sticks

MARINADE
30 ml lime juice
30 ml lime zest
2 red chillies, deseeded and finely sliced
10 ml cumin seeds
10 ml sesame oil

SALAD
30 ml caramel sugar
30 ml lime juice
2 green mangoes, peeled and cut into matchsticks (reserve all the juice)
4 shallots, cleaned and thinly sliced on the diagonal
2 red chillies, deseeded and thinly sliced
a handful of fresh mint leaves, chopped
a small bunch of fresh coriander leaves

Mix all the marinade ingredients together. (Only marinate the prawns about 10 minutes before you are ready to grill them.)

To make the salad, dissolve the sugar in the lime juice. Toss the mangoes, shallots and chillies in the sugar-lime juice dressing and scatter the mint and coriander leaves over.

Marinate the prawns for 10 minutes, then skewer them onto kebab sticks (2 per stick). Grill them 1 minute per side in a ridged grill pan or under an oven grill.

Dish the salad into 4 individual serving bowls and top with 2 prawn kebabs each. Serves 4 as a starter

Mary Mary Quite Contrary

The fruit and vegetable market in Büyükada on Princes' Islands, Turkey (left).

Like Mary, I love gardening. And like my father, I love vegetable gardening. Wherever we moved, one could go by his radish clock. Within 14 days of our arrival, Dad would present us with his first miniscule radishes and the comment, 'Just thinning them out.'

So it happened that working at Villa Athena in Skiathos, Greece, I felt the need to establish a vegetable garden. When Yannis heard of my very tentative plan, he was most enthusiastic. So enthusiastic that he offered three black fig trees as backbone in the layout. He arrived with a mechanical digger, the trees, compost and manure. The planting was done in no time. There was no going back so Veron, an Albanian friend, and I set to cleaning the area under the trees and the local plant nursery supplied sturdy seedlings of aubergines, tomatoes, sweet peppers and basil. After tilling the shady soil with compost and manure, we planted them in neat rows around the trees. In a very short time, we noticed little tomatoes, aubergines and peppers forming. The more basil we picked, the wilder the bushes grew. Soon we had more veggies than we could use. Mary would have been proud of our garden's growth. We encouraged the guests from Villa Athena's self-catering units to harvest vegetables as they needed them.

An Italian family came to stay in the summer of 2001. Lovely young parents with a bright five-year-old son. Growing up in the city of Milan does not allow for an agricultural education. When we mentioned the vegetable patch they were delighted. They set a pattern: restaurant dinner one night, home-cooking the next, at which time little Marco could decide what he would like for dinner. He and his Dad would walk to the vegetable garden and harvest their own supper. He also learnt how to prepare salads, how to stuff a pepper and all the things that a good Italian should know.

Our remarkable harvest soon had us experimenting: 100 ways with sweet peppers, 150 ways with tomatoes and 200 ways with aubergines! We prepared various ratatouilles, different moussakas, some aubergine salads, sweet peppers in oil, sundried tomatoes in oil, aubergines in oil. Our endeavours constantly opened new horizons. Often, in exchange for a basket of shiny baby aubergines, a sun-ripened tomato and green, yellow and red peppers, we were offered family recipes. All most successful.

The old Greek kitchen, open to guests, has all but disappeared. The cook, sometimes *yia-yia*, sometimes mama or an aunt, would proudly lift lids: *stifado* (beef stew), *yiouvetsi* (meat with tomatoes), *arni me patates* (roast lamb), *avgolemono* soup (made with egg and lemon juice) … What to choose? I was usually swayed by the large baking dishes of stuffed peppers, stuffed tomatoes and *papoutsakia* (little shoes), a most appropriate name for halved aubergines, generously filled with a rich tomato sauce, packed in neat rows and slowly cooked in the oven until caramelly and treacly, the aroma heady and tempting. And that is where the Turkish name for this dish originates: *Imam Bayildi* (the Imam swooned). Each time a cook prepared the dish for the learned man, the aroma, floating ahead and heralding its appearance, excited him beyond endurance and induced a swoon.

Lennie's seedlings (above), and (below) Sylvia, Marco and Guido Sibona, our Italian guests at Villa Athena, Skiathos.

STUFFED TOMATOES AND PEPPERS

Yiorgos and Eleni's sons are typical of well-balanced, refined young Greek men. We are ever so proud to name this tightly knit family from Thessalonica among our friends. It was a bitter blow when Eleni was diagnosed with, and sadly succumbed to cancer. Her legacy of keeping the family together with love and good cooking is proudly continued by Yannis, Theodoros, Polina (Theodoros's wife) and Thanasis. Yannis plays the cello in the State Symphony Orchestra of Thessaloniki, Theodorus and Polina run the family business and Thanos works for a bank. They all love food and though I was quite prepared to sit with a Greek recipe and a dictionary, they provided me with a translation of Eleni's recipe.

enough ripe but firm tomatoes and green peppers to fill a large baking pan
olive oil
2 onions, chopped
cloves garlic to taste, finely chopped
salt and freshly ground black pepper to taste
a generous bunch of fresh parsley, chopped
15 ml uncooked rice per tomato and pepper

The brothers Stefos: Yannis, Theodoris and Thanasis from Thessalonika.

Preheat the oven to 180 °C.

Cut the tops off the tomatoes and green peppers (but retain as lids). Discard the pepper seeds and scoop out the tomato pulp, but keep for the stuffing. Pack the tomatoes and peppers tightly into a baking pan.

Pour sufficient olive oil into a saucepan to cover its base, then place over a medium heat. Braise the onions until golden brown and soft. Add the garlic and cook for a few seconds. Add the tomato pulp, salt and pepper, parsley and rice. Bring to the boil and parboil until the rice is just a little tender but not yet expanding.

Place a spoon of rice mixture into each tomato and pepper and cover with its 'lid'. Turn upside down in the baking pan, keeping the lids in place. Pour some olive oil over them (enough to cover the base of the pan) as well as about 375 ml water. Bake in the oven for about 25 minutes, adding water occasionally to allow for absorption by the rice as well as evaporation.

Remove from the oven and turn the tomatoes and peppers over again so that the lids are on top. Add more water to keep them moist and bake for a further 25 minutes. At the end, the rice should be fully cooked and tender, and the tomatoes and peppers still whole and juicy.

Any extra rice may be cooked alongside the tomatoes and peppers in the pan and used as top-up filling for those that are not full enough. The addition of minced meat (lamb and/or pork) is common, but makes for a heavier dish. Serves ±8 as a main course

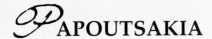APOUTSAKIA

6 small brinjals (aubergines), stems trimmed
125 ml olive oil
2 large onions, sliced
2 cloves garlic, crushed
1 x 400 g can tomato passata (rich tomato purée)
a handful of fresh flat-leaf parsley, chopped
salt and freshly ground black pepper to taste
5 ml sugar
125 ml lemon juice

Preheat the oven to 180 °C.

Peel the brinjals in strips, leaving alternate strips of skin on. Heat a little of the oil in a frying pan. Fry the brinjals whole, turning them all the while in order to brown them. Leave to cool. Cut them in half lengthways. Using a spoon or melon scoop, remove some of the flesh, leaving a perfect shell to be filled later. Reserve the scooped-out flesh.

Pour the rest of the oil into a saucepan and braise the onions until soft and golden brown. Add the garlic and cook briefly. Add the scooped-out flesh, tomatoes, parsley and salt and pepper. Cook for about 15 minutes, stirring from time to time. Remove from the heat.

Fill the shells with the tomato mixture, then pack them tightly into a baking dish. Combine the sugar and lemon juice, then drizzle over the *papoutsakia*. Cover the dish with a lid or heavy aluminium foil and bake for approximately 15 minutes, or until the juices have reduced to a syrupy consistency.

Serve at room temperature. This dish improves if it stands for 1–2 days. Serves 6 as a main course or 12 as a side dish

ᒪ OURGETTE MASH
with roasted cherry tomatoes

500 g cherry tomatoes

60 ml olive oil

2 cloves garlic, crushed

salt and freshly ground black pepper
  to taste

cayenne pepper (optional)

500 g courgettes, cut into chunks

125 ml water

a generous quantity of fresh Italian
  flat-leaf parsley, chopped

Preheat the oven to 180 °C.

Arrange the tomatoes on a baking tray, moisten with a little olive oil and sprinkle over the crushed garlic. Season with a little salt and pepper. (If you like, you could add the tiniest sprinkling of cayenne pepper.) Bake for 30 minutes. Remove from the oven and leave to cool.

Heat a little more olive oil in a saucepan and stir-fry the courgettes for 1–2 minutes. Do not brown them. Pour in the water and cook until really tender. Add more water if necessary, but rather allow the water to boil away. Remove from the heat and drain very well. Mash the courgettes with a fork or masher, then mix in the parsley. Turn into a shallow dish and form a hollow in the centre for the tomatoes. Place the tomatoes in the hollow.

Serve at room temperature. Serves 6 as a side dish

ℓ OURGETTES
with sultanas and pine nuts

60 ml olive oil
500 g courgettes, sliced into bâtons
30 ml sultanas
1 clove garlic, crushed
salt and freshly ground black pepper
  to taste
30 ml pine nuts, toasted
10–12 fresh mint leaves, torn lengthways
lemon wedges to serve

Heat the oil in a frying pan and fry the courgettes rapidly, taking care not to over-cook them; they must still be slightly crispy. Add the sultanas and garlic and cook for 30 seconds. Season with salt and pepper. Remove from the heat and pour into a shallow dish. Leave to cool to room temperature. Sprinkle with the pine nuts.

Serve with a scattering of mint leaves and lemon wedges on the side. Serves 6 as a side dish

SALUT
DE
CONSTANTINOPLE

Palais Impérial de Dolma-Bagtché

Iles des Princes, Prinkipo.

Salut de Constantinople.

Vintage Turkish postcards

And the Cow Jumped Over the Moon

An oil painting purchased in Cairo (above), and a vintage Turkish postcard of a lemonade vendor (right).

No. 39. Smyrne — Marchand de Limonade

16·4
07.

Sisters Hanli Morreira and Marga Le Clerc at the Topkapi Palace, Istanbul, 1970 (top), and (bottom) a vintage Turkish postcard of an odalisque (a female slave).

Late in the summer of 1970, Hanli, Marga and I drove from northern Greece into Turkey, crossing the border at Idirne. Relations between the two countries were strained and we were apprehensive. The Turkish officials asked to see our visas. We had none. The Turkish Consulate in Athens had assured me that visas were not required. The commander of the border post was not there and he was the only decision maker. We were told he would only be back the next day.

Thank goodness for the girls! They persuaded the officials and our passports were stamped '*Dikkat!*' The bearer of this passport must pay a fine of x amount upon leaving the country.'

In the meanwhile we met another South African, a young man in the same predicament. We offered him a lift to Istanbul. It rapidly became dark and we decided to stay at a camp site rather than drive into an unknown city at night. The girls slept in the back of the Volkswagen Variant, while I slept outside, alongside our belongings, food and water. Fearing a chilly night, I changed into a tracksuit, snuggled into my sleeping bag and buried myself under a *flokati* rug. Our new friend climbed into the flimsiest of sleeping bags that he had bought in Belgium and which, he claimed, could keep one warm in the Antarctic!

I slept uneasily. Was the young man safe in this weather? The girls and I awoke early. He was still asleep. We completed our ablutions, packed the car and began to worry. He hadn't moved and his moustache was white with frost. What would we tell his parents if … ? How would we locate them? Was he breathing?

He woke up, well rested and ready for the day. Why do we torture ourselves so?

We drove to the Blue Mosque where our Istanbul adventure started. The following morning our hiker friend contacted us to thank us and to invite us to a mystery treat. It was a dreary, rainy day. As he quickly walked us to our destination, we got wet and muddy along the busy sidewalks of old Istanbul, and could only steal the odd glance at buildings, shops and stalls on the way. One restaurant caught my eye with its curved glass windows, cracking old-gold signage, marble floors, wood-and-brass fittings, Art Nouveau tables with marble tops, a long counter covered in sweet things and the aroma of coffee in the air. Our leader stopped at the main door and ushered us in. At last we sat down. There was no need to order as our host strolled over and spoke to the staff. Minutes later milky drinks arrived, attractive in tall glasses encased in metal frames with handles.

'*Melkkos*, Turkish *melkkos*!' he announced.

What a treat! We were surprised and delighted. He had, by chance, discovered this treat called *sahleb* there, but which is known in South Africa as *melkkos* (milk food). A thickening agent made from ground orchid bulbs – not unlike cornflour or orris root – forms the basis of this milky drink. It is further enhanced with sugar and spices such as cinnamon and cardamom, as well as rose-water and chopped pistachios. Recipes differ from place to place. That dreary Istanbul morning became memorable as we sipped hot ambrosia in an environment light-years away from our norm. We enjoyed every drop as the long spoons helped us retrieve every pistachio chip from the bottoms of the glasses.

———✸———

In the cool Egyptian winter of 1997, while in Zamalek on our umpteenth trip to Cairo, we decided to visit the Coptic Quarter. Walking along the Cairean sidewalks can be trying. Crossing the three-made-into-five-lane streets is a definite threat to one's sanity. We were about to order a taxi when I noticed an old woman wrapped in miles of cloth. 'They won't flatten her!' We rushed over to her, all but clung to her skirts and … crossed safely.

From Tahrir Square we took the metro to *Mari Girgis* (Holy Mary) where we visited the Christian churches, museums and the place where Mary and Joseph are purported to have lain the Christ child down. It was a lovely, tranquil visit after the chaotic Cairean roads. Afterwards, we lingered on a little square enjoying the relative silence. It was chilly to be out, but the desert air was invigorating. I looked up at a menu, crudely written, above a little refreshment kiosk. There it was: *Sahleb*. Since we first met, poor Lennie had been tortured with my Istanbul *sahleb* story. He had never tasted it, so that was our chance.

Going back, seeing again, tasting once more … it does not always work, but I was prepared to take the chance. After all, a little stony square in *Mari Girgis* is not a faded but chic sweet shop in Istanbul. Little Egyptian glasses that burn your hands are not Art Noveau treasures. But sipping hot *sahleb* ambrosia again, Lennie for the first time, we were transported to the little heaven of *Mari Girgis*. The lovely spices, the nuts, the rich milkyness – it was all there. Our friend Khaled found us some *sahleb* powder – the very best – and we brought it home to Cape Town. *Sahleb* travels well, freezes well and transports one to far-away places and dream worlds.

———✸———

'Bazaars' seem to have lost favour. There used to be church bazaars, school bazaars, W.A. bazaars, hospice bazaars. Thank goodness they were staggered, making it possible to attend them all in turn. I loved the luncheons with my parents, the craft tables, the cupcake stands, the tombola, the raffles and the pudding table with rows of little pudding bowls, each with three or four scoops of different puddings. They were sold systematically from one end to the other. My agenda was always to try for a dish that contained snow pudding and stone pudding – and a lot of custard. The trick was to linger until those bowls came up in the system and then to jump the queue. A sweetly smiling boy, so enthusiastic about his pudding, always got away with such behaviour!

Every now and then one of our dairy farmer friends supplied us with milk, which arrived in genuine half-gallon, metal milk pails with recessed lids, cool from the milk shed. This usually heralded a special treat: Mom would make a large jar of sweet, runny custard and place it in the fridge. After school we would make a bee-line for the cool custard, which we drank by the glass. It was not a sophisticated egg custard. Mom used Bird's custard powder and even today that is what I reach for.

Covered Bazaar, Istanbul.

ISTANBUL

$\mathcal{M}$Y VERSION OF SAHLEB

Sahleb, *the powdered root of an orchid species, has become very expensive, and as it's also so difficult to source, I have resorted to using cornflour.*

25 ml cornflour
500 ml milk
15 ml ground pistachios
3 ml cardamom seeds, ground in a mortar and pestle
15 ml fine desiccated coconut
30 ml sugar
ground cinnamon and ground pistachios to sprinkle
grated nutmeg to sprinkle (optional)

Mix the cornflour into half a cup (125 ml) of milk. In a saucepan, bring the rest of the milk to the boil. Add a little of the boiling milk to the cornflour mixture, stirring vigorously. Pour this mixture into the boiling milk and keep on stirring, while it returns to boiling point. It will thicken within a few minutes.

Stir in the pistachios, ground cardamom, coconut and sugar. Pour into glasses with handles (or cups) and sprinkle with a little cinnamon and some pistachios. I also love to grate a little nutmeg over mine. Serves 6

Orchids in our entrance hall (top), Coptic crosses for sale in Mari Girgis, Cairo *(centre), and waiting for steaming hot sahleb in* Mari Girgis, Cairo's *coptic area (left).*

AULIFLOWER SOUP

75 g butter
1 large onion, chopped
5 ml ground coriander
5 ml ground cumin
15 ml grated fresh ginger
1 clove garlic, crushed
500 g cauliflower florets, without the thickest stems
1 large potato, peeled and chopped
500 ml vegetable stock
500 ml milk
3 fresh bay leaves
salt and freshly ground black pepper to taste
sour cream, paprika oil and 6 fresh bay leaves to garnish

Melt the butter in a saucepan and braise the onion until translucent and tender but not brown. Stir in the coriander, cumin, ginger and garlic and braise for a few minutes. Add the cauliflower, potato, stock, milk and 3 bay leaves. Bring to the boil and simmer, uncovered, until the vegetables are tender. Discard the bay leaves, leave to cool slightly, then blend in a food processor until smooth. Season to taste.

Serve hot with a dollop of sour cream and paprika oil. Garnish with a bay leaf. Serves 6 as a starter

A roof terrace breakfast of morning pancakes in Essaouira, Morocco.

He Stuck a Feather in his Cap and Called it Macaroni

Just recently I learnt that the beautiful, large, terracotta pots in which the nuns of Santa Maria Novella in Florence cure their fragrant pot-pourri come from Imprunetta. Our friends Amedeo and Emma drove us there for lunch. We stopped at the potteries along the way and wished both for lots of money and a good transport firm! From there we drove to the centre of the not-so-pretty town to look for a particular *osteria* (small restaurant) noted in Emma's little book. Obliging municipal officials provided us with directions and told us that it was a really good restaurant.

Tucked away in a side street, the building was hardly attractive. On the terrace in front there were some of those all-in-one eight-seater bench and table structures. We looked again. Yes, it *was* the good eatery, Lo Ziro. Our Italian friends barged in and we followed timidly. Once inside we were fascinated. Through the open kitchen doors we could see a young woman flitting about. Her dark hair was scraped back in a ponytail and her already very white cheeks were matte with dustings of flour. Chef Maurizio was in charge, serving, taking orders, advising, laying tables, dispensing olive oil and singing the odd opera aria at full volume. A wedding party of about 20 guests was enjoying a jolly luncheon at the other end of the room.

Chef Maurizio was obviously a singular character. His black-and-white chef's trousers were printed with a bright array of red, yellow and green peppers, his feet were clad in a comfortable pair of orange clogs. His white chef's jacket and hat framed his jolly face from where a bright orange goatee extended in an upward curve.

It was easy to establish a rapport with him if you remembered that it was his restaurant and that he made the jokes. As he passed our table on the way to the wedding party with a large platter piled high with deep-fried calamari, Amedeo asked, 'Oh, what is that?'

Maurizio either did not answer or we could not hear. On his way back, Amedeo tried again, 'Is that on the menu?'

'No! We do not do deep-frying here!' replied Maurizio. Perplexed, we wondered what it was, then. But on his next trip from the kitchen, he nonchalantly placed a big cone, fashioned out of a paper placemat, brimful of calamari, onto our table. An inelegant scramble ensued!

We ordered various types of pasta from Maurizio. I am generally not fond of pastas with creamy sauces, so I ordered the simplest: fresh tomato and basil. Others preferred spaghetti carbonara, penne arrabiata and a penne with mushroom sauce. Lennie had no fewer than three starters, not able to decide on one! How the little flour-faced woman managed it, I do not know, but our pastas all arrived at the same time, perfectly *al dente*, hot and delicious. On the shelves next to our table were rows of bottles of olive oil. We had assumed they were for sale, but as Maurizio placed the dishes in front of us he turned

HE STUCK A FEATHER IN HIS CAP AND CALLED IT MACARONI

to the shelves, hesitated, then selected the right oil for each of our dishes. Peppery or smooth, green or golden – they all came from some corner of Italy specifically to flavour our pasta dishes.

———

Learning from the masters requires an open mind, a readiness to accept and absorb, patience and humility. All of these come easily when your 'master' is Lina. She simply tells stories and anecdotes, and your mind follows, transporting you to her Italian mother-in-law's kitchen, the garden, the market. You find out when to pick fruit, how to ripen the tomatoes on the windowsill, how many pinches to use … and how to guard your pasta. Never leave it alone! With the various products on the market, it has become apparent to me that no two pastas have the same cooking time. The ten minutes of yesterday's pasta may be five too many for today's offering. So I now stay with my pasta, watch and test frequently. Lina also explained why pasta comes in so many shapes. It has everything to do with the accompanying sauces. Shell pasta explains it best if you imagine the hollows capturing a lovely light sauce. *Linguini,* however, holds rich flavoursome tomato sauces well. I love using *farfalle* with flat pieces of smoked salmon and sour cream. *Fettuccini* and a mushroom sauce seem to be friends.

When we were in Puglia, it seemed, after a while, that there was no getting away from *orechietti,* literally meaning 'little ears'. It was high summer and we were rather concerned at the not-so-summery *orechietti* dishes we encountered everywhere, usually served with very rich sauces, each and every little 'ear' brimful. But a welcome offering down south were the little dishes of crisply fried breadcrumbs with various dishes, but especially with pastas. On one occasion we were served a lovely dish of tubertina with tomato, cubes of fish and a bowl of golden crumbs. Another delicacy was oven-baked potato with bacon, cheese and crumbs.

We got to know another master of Italian cooking, Frank Swainston, and his legendary food at Constantia Uitsig. His tomato sauce was sublime, particularly when served with his *crespelle di verdura* (vegetable pancakes). He revealed the secret: slow stew-cooking and the addition of carrot and celery. This has become my stock tomato sauce. Frank introduced me to *crespelle* (pancakes), and while he rolled them with fillings to make roulade, I enjoy forming a stacked cake.

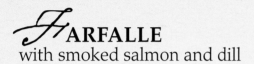FARFALLE
with smoked salmon and dill

I honestly don't remember where I found this recipe, but our friends know it will be on the menu if they arrive unexpectedly. And I daresay, it's a special treat, bearing in mind their temporary lack of courtesy!

500 g farfalle
200 g smoked salmon, cut into small pieces
50 g fresh dill, chopped
100 g freshly grated Parmesan cheese
250 ml sour cream
salt and freshly ground black pepper to taste
olive oil to drizzle
shavings of Parmesan cheese to garnish

In a saucepan, boil the farfalle in plenty of salted water until *al dente*.

In the meanwhile, assemble all the remaining ingredients and warm the serving plates or bowls in readiness. As soon as the farfalle is ready, drain it and immediately return to the hot saucepan.

Over a very low heat, add all the ingredients to the piping hot pasta and stir through thoroughly. Remove from the heat and serve in the warm dishes. Top with a drizzle of olive oil and a few shavings of Parmesan cheese. Serves 4 as a main course

HE STUCK A FEATHER IN HIS CAP AND CALLED IT MACARONI

CRESPELLE DI VERDURA

PANCAKES
6 eggs
400 ml milk
140 g cake flour
20 ml olive oil
salt to taste
melted butter for brushing
grated Parmesan cheese
    to sprinkle
tomato sauce to serve
    (homemade is good)

FILLING 1
500 g leeks, well rinsed and
    sliced
45 ml olive oil
a knob of butter

FILLING 2
500 g spinach or silver beet
45 ml olive oil
a knob of butter
500 g ricotta cheese
freshly grated nutmeg
salt and pepper to taste

FILLING 3
1 kg butternut
15 ml olive oil
salt and pepper to taste

CRUMBS
1 sour dough (or similar) bread,
    crumbled
olive oil
spices or dried herbs (optional)

For the pancakes, mix the eggs, milk, flour, oil and salt together and leave to rest for at least 1 hour. Cook the pancakes in the traditional manner in a frying pan, stacking them as you go.

To make filling 1, stew the leeks in the oil and butter until tender.

For filling 2, wash the spinach well and shake dry. Chop roughly. Heat the oil and butter in a large saucepan and drop in the spinach. Allow it to wilt then remove from the saucepan. If any juice has formed, reduce it to a thick sauce then add to the spinach. Mix in the ricotta, nutmeg, salt and pepper.

To make filling 3, preheat the oven to 180 °C. Peel and depip the butternut, then cut into cubes. Place the cubes in a mixing bowl, add the oil and salt and pepper. Toss to cover all the cubes with the oil. Spread them on a baking tray and bake for 30 minutes or until tender and perhaps slightly brown. Leave to cool slightly, then mash roughly.

Spread the first pancake with filling 1 (the leeks) and cover with a second pancake. Spread some of the spinach mixture over, then cover with a third pancake. Onto that spread some of the butternut and cover with a fourth pancake. Continue with these layers until you have used up all the fillings. Press down lightly on the 'cake' using a board, a plate or a cake tin. Take care not to press too hard, causing the filling to ooze out!

For the crumbs, crumble the bread and moisten the crumbs with some olive oil. Spices or dried herbs may also be sprinkled over the crumbs, if you like. Spread the crumbs onto a baking sheet and bake in the oven at 180 °C until golden brown. They catch quickly so watch them carefully.

This cake may be served whole or in slices, but either way it is better if heated. Set the oven to 180 °C. Brush the top of the cake (or slices) amply with the butter and sprinkle with Parmesan and the prepared crumbs. Place in the oven for 20 minutes or until golden brown. Serve with a tomato sauce. Serves 6 as a main course

MY TOMATO SAUCE

1 large onion, chopped	1 x 30–40 g can tomato paste
2 sticks celery, chopped	15 ml honey
1 carrot, grated	1 red chilli, deseeded and chopped
50 ml olive oil	400 ml water
2 x 400 g cans chopped tomatoes	salt and freshly ground black pepper to taste

In a large saucepan, braise the onion, celery and carrot in the olive oil until lightly browned. Add the chopped tomatoes, the tomato paste, honey, chilli and water. Turn the heat to medium and simmer, stirring frequently, until the carrot and celery are tender. If the mixture thickens too quickly, add more water. The longer the sauce simmers, the richer the taste. Finally, season with the salt and pepper. Keep refrigerated. Makes ±1 litre

They Sang him a Ballad and Fed him on Salad

A real Greek salad in the garden at Villa Ella, Skiathos (top left), a summer salad for lunch in Marrakech, Morocco (top right), and (bottom) Kastro Beach, Skiathos, Greece.

Ask for a Greek salad anywhere – with the exception of Greece – and you will get a bed of lettuce, slices of tomato, little blocks of feta cheese, slices of cucumber, pitted olives and onion rings. The dressing? A creamy, perfect emulsion.

The 'Greek' Greek salads that we enjoyed, looked and tasted quite different. Definitely no green leaves! Tomatoes and cucumber were invariably chopped into large segments, the olives farm-style without added lemons or herbs and still with their pips. Onions were sliced, but generally not in rings. Surmounting the lot was a slab of feta (neither creamy nor hard and crumbly) and a puddle of lovely green olive oil dribbled from the feta into the vegetables. When we lived on Skiathos, this was the salad we had for lunch every day, teamed with the morning's bread. At the end of each meal we would savour a morsel of bread with which we wiped up the last drop of olive oil, fragrant with tomato and cucumber juices.

In Greece, such a salad is called a peasant salad, *horiatiki salata*. Should you order the same in Cyprus, you're most likely to find it served on a bed of thinly sliced cabbage. We soon got into this habit as well!

The term 'salad' becomes *really* confusing when one is served a hot potato salad or a boiled carrot salad. As far back as the 1980s we were given a recipe for hot chicken salad, which we fed to all and sundry, at any time, day or night. Aubergines incinerated over coals, washed to remove the ashes of the skins, then pulped and mixed with crushed garlic, lemon juice and olive oil, is a salad. A delicious one!

In the '60s there was an alarming trend to set grated carrots or grated cooked beetroot in jellies in ring moulds. They were often served with plain lettuce leaves or watercress. A side dish of mayonnaise was also a regular accompaniment. To save oneself from the sweet jellied moulds, there are always the classic salads: Waldorf, Niçoise, Russian, Caesar … but they need to be put together expertly. Consequently, I most enjoy the spontaneous 'whatever is in the fridge or growing in the garden' kind of salad.

As I write, I can still taste this evening's salad: a dressing of sweet mustard sauce, lime juice, olive oil, salt and pepper; into that a grated (Granny Smith) apple and some thinly sliced chives and gherkin. On top of it all was a handful of watercress and rocket. Just before serving, the salad was tossed and the leaves coated with the dressing, chives and apple. That's what was in the fridge and it was deeeelicious!

Lunch at Kastro on Skiathos (top), salads for a Greek Easter lunch feast in Almyros, Greece (centre), and (bottom) lunch of wild greens and home-grown vegetables in Peliou, mainland Greece.

THEY SANG HIM A BALLAD AND FED HIM ON SALAD | *139*

BRINJAL AND CHICKPEA SALAD

2 medium brinjals (aubergines), topped and tailed
1 large red onion, cut into thin wedges
5 ml ground coriander
5 ml ground cumin
1 fresh red chilli, deseeded and sliced
60 ml olive oil (plus a little more)
500 g spinach, washed and dried
1 x 400 g can chickpeas, drained
1 lemon
fresh coriander leaves to garnish
thick plain yoghurt or labnah cheese balls to serve

Preheat the oven to 180 °C.

Cut the brinjals into 2-cm cubes. Place them, with the onion wedges, in a mixing bowl. Sprinkle with the coriander, cumin, chilli and 60 ml olive oil. Toss well in order to cover all the brinjals and onion with the mixture. Spread the vegetables in a baking tray and bake for 30–35 minutes, until tender but not too soft.

Remove any large stalks from the spinach. Heat a little olive oil in a saucepan, then drop in the spinach and stir, wilting the leaves, but not cooking it to a limp mush. Drain and turn the leaves out onto a cutting board and chop them roughly.

In a large bowl, mix the brinjals and onions, chickpeas and wilted spinach together. Squeeze the lemon over the salad. If you wish, you could first zest the lemon and scatter over the salad before squeezing over the juice. Garnish the salad with coriander and serve with a bowl of yoghurt or some *labnah* balls. Serves 4 as a side dish

A quiet moment on the rooftop terrace at Dar Les Cigognes hotel, Marrakech.

COOKED CARROT SALAD

It is astounding that such a humble vegetable can become so delicious with only the addition of a few spices!

10 ml cumin seeds
10 ml coriander seeds
500 g very fresh crisp carrots, peeled
harissa or chilli paste to your taste
60 ml wine- or cider-vinegar
60 ml good quality olive oil
2–3 cloves garlic, chopped or crushed
±2.5-cm piece fresh ginger, grated
black olives or sprigs of celery to garnish

Dry-fry the cumin and coriander seeds in a pan, taking care not to burn them, then pound them in a mortar.

Boil the carrots in salted water to soften them. Drain, then mash them with a potato masher. Mix in the rest of the ingredients (except the olives) and leave to stand awhile, for the flavours to blend. (You could purée in a blender if you prefer, but I prefer the 'crushed' purée mixture.)

Spoon into a serving dish, building it into a tower and dot with juicy black olives and garnish with celery. Serve with a flatbread or crisp lettuce leaves. Serves 6 as a side dish

THEY SANG HIM A BALLAD AND FED HIM ON SALAD

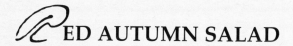

RED AUTUMN SALAD

This salad changes all the time as I use any red produce I can lay my hands on. I think, though, this one takes the Red Onion Award!

1 red onion, thinly sliced and macerated
   in lemon juice
1 red pepper, cut into matchsticks
2 blush-red apples (preferably the
   perfumed Fuji variety), sliced
6 whole baby beetroot (1 per plate
   (if you feel brave)
2 pillowpacks Italian salad leaves
   (with deep-red radicchio leaves)
75 g cranberry jelly, cut into 1-cm slices,
   then cubed
a sprinkling of pink peppercorns

DRESSING
80 ml balsamic reduction glaze
125 ml olive oil
a pinch of salt
freshly ground black pepper

Combine the dressing ingredients. Arrange the salad ingredients attractively in a serving dish and drizzle with the dressing.
Serves 6 as a side dish

The Princess and the Pea

We were dying to know whether Capri was really as wonderful as everybody said it was.

In the summer of 1994 we set off from Greece to visit our dear South African-Greek friend Antigone and her husband, Alfredo, originally from Naples. The trip there was awe-inspiring. We took the funicular to the top of the island – where Antigone was waiting to greet us. It was so good to see her again; it was unbelievable that we should be on her home ground!

Once a porter had transferred our luggage to their home, we were taken on an orientation walk. Antigone bought cheese from her regular fromagerie – a cave-like shop, smelling clearly of all the many cheeses on display. We were invited to taste a few of them. Then the bakery, the fish shop and the *salumeria* (the general dealer). We had arrived in gourmet heaven.

At that point – and this was a bit unexpected – Antigone asked us how long we were staying. 'Until Saturday morning,' we replied.

'No, no,' she exclaimed. (At this point we were concerned that we were overstaying our welcome.) She explained that she had gone to a lot of trouble to procure two invitations to the best party of the season – at Katherine Mondadori's. We had to stay until at least Sunday. Phew! But a whole new problem surfaced … the nothing-to-wear-complication. Antigone sorted that out rapidly: do you have neat trousers, neat shirts, pullovers that you can tie over your shoulders? Yes. Italian chic.

On the night of the party we hesitantly walked up to an imposing gate and were duly invited in upon presentation of our invitations. Beyond the stone walls, which we had come to know from passing by on our daily walks into the village, lay a wonderland of terraced gardens, gazebos, pools and a home so inviting that we felt comfortable from the word go. There were many people, and an unbelievable variety. In fact, on discovering that we were to be seated at different tables, Lennie had a minor panic attack and feigned a migraine or threatened to jump from the first terrace.

A party on the island of Capri (top), Lennie with Gary Keener in Capri, 1994 (centre), and (bottom) Johan with the Milanese horse breeder.

At dinner I was seated at a table with an elegant horse breeder woman from Milan, as well as the mayor of Capri and an array of people who spoke no intelligible language. Lennie, at his table, sat next to movie director Lina Wertmüller, a Milanese designer who had fashioned the table flowers for the evening, a well-known Italian comic actor and a young Hawaiian from Laguna Beach, Gary Keener.

Walking through the house we were fascinated by two beautiful wall hangings of dried plant material, old gardening implements and a collection of bleached driftwood and other found objects. They were the work of the London floral artist, Kenneth Turner.

146   THE PRINCESS AND THE PEA

In the entrance hall there was an extremely high stack of many beautifully made, brightly coloured mattresses. This was an installation by a favourite artist of the hostess and it was named 'The Princess and the Pea'!

And by the way, Capri was even better than we'd been told.

Pea soup in winter – what could be better? Bean soup, perhaps, or lentil soup?

⟨∞⟩

Travelling across the Greek mainland from Ioannina, south of the mountains, towards Kozani, we stopped in Metsovo. It was the end of the summer season, a chilly day and a light mist was mingling with wood-fire smoke in the treetops. Known for its excellent cheeses – notably the smoked variety – the town also sported a number of small shops selling textiles woven in the area. The lovely piece we were interested in, we were told, was a museum piece. It was obviously old, beautifully coloured and just a teeny bit frayed. We bought it at a fair price, but all the bargaining made us very thirsty, and hungry!

We found a cosy little tavern from where a tantalising fragrance wafted. Never having had real winter soup in Greece the idea was rather odd and we presumed the kitchen was preparing *stifado* (beef stew) or a lamb dish. Casually we asked the waiter whether they had any soup on the menu – only to be surprised by his '*Malista*! (of course), Metsovo is also known for the best bean soup in the country'.

They could well be proud of the soup that day. It was served with crusty fresh bread and smoked cheese. A pleasant local wine complemented the meal and our impression of the little village became rosier with every sip. We were sad to leave, but as we headed off to Thessalonika, the car was fragrant with the smell of bread and smoked cheese. We had bought a whole cheese, oddly but traditionally shaped like an elongated butternut squash. Yannis's family was overawed by the gift of the cheese and bread from Metsovo. It was so highly prized elsewhere. For us it was a joy to see our gift so genuinely appreciated.

I must admit that soups made by other people invariably taste better than my own. Yet, our masala pea soup is quick and easy to make and scrumptious!

⟨∞⟩

It was quite by chance that we ended up staying at the Sheraton Hotel on the Shari el Nil in Dokki, Cairo. There is a coffee shop on the ground floor where they serve coffee, pastries and other sweet things all day long, as well as good lunches and suppers. The views are limited to people using the lifts and the guests at the coffee shop. The other side of the building boasted a lovely view of the Nile. One day a board proclaimed that the special of the day was *khosari*. Upon enquiring we discovered that it was a rice, lentil and fried onion dish. We hesitated, thinking it rather plain, but were eventually swayed by the fact that it was totally vegetarian, and that we love rice and lentils. Well, that experience saw us going back for more, again and again. We had also grown accustomed to the view.

Our faithful old Italian greyhouse, Jasper, making himself at home on the 'museum piece' cushion from Metsovo!

PEA SOUP
with garam masala

1 large onion, chopped
sunflower oil
3 ml garam masala
750 ml flavourful vegetable stock
  (see below for home-made)
500 g frozen peas
salt and freshly ground black pepper
  to taste

Braise the onion in the oil until soft, but
still pale. Add the garam masala and cook
for a few minutes to release the flavour.
Drench with the stock and add the peas.
Boil until they are quite tender. Leave to
cool somewhat.

Liquidise the soup mixture or pass it
through a sieve, then season to taste. This
simple soup may be garnished according to
your preference, e.g. sour cream, mint jelly,
crispy bits of bacon or croutons sprinkled
with paprika. Serves 6 as a starter

HOMEMADE VEGETABLE STOCK
1 stick celery, chopped
2 medium carrots, chopped
a few stalks of parsley
1 large leek, chopped
1 litre water

Boil all the ingredients together for
approximately 30 minutes, then strain.
Makes ±750 ml

*M*EATBALLS
with chickpeas and spinach

MEATBALLS
2 slices white bread
750 g beef, lamb or pork, or a mixture –
  finely minced
2 eggs, lightly beaten
2 ml ground allspice
salt and pepper
flour for coating
sunflower oil for frying

CHICKPEAS AND SPINACH
a knob of butter
500 g spinach, washed, stalks removed
  and roughly chopped
1 x 400 g can chickpeas, drained
salt and pepper to taste
fresh mint leaves to garnish

Soak the bread in water, squeeze dry and crumble. Mix together the bread, meat, eggs and seasoning, then pound or knead for a while to create a fine, smooth texture. Shape the mixture into walnut-sized balls and roll them in flour. Fry in a little oil until brown all over.

Heat the butter in a saucepan and add the spinach. Stir while it wilts in its own liquid. Do not cover. Add the chickpeas to the spinach, then season with salt and pepper. Bury the meatballs in the mixture and simmer for about 30 minutes.

Turn out into a shallow serving dish and garnish with torn mint leaves. Serve with thick yoghurt on the side. Serves 6 as a side dish

*Egyptian women baking aish baladi (flat breads)
in Cairo (top and bottom), and (centre) a pretzel
vendor in Emenönü, Istanbul.*

Pat-a-cake,
Pat-a-cake,
Bakers man

Moroccan breakfast pastries ready to be baked (top), and Greek confectionery (bottom).

There used to be a charming ladies' fashion boutique in Regent Road, Sea Point, at a time when little galleries, fashion accessories shops and interesting restaurants proliferated along there. The two lady proprietors ran their shop personally, proudly offering beautifully crafted garments that Lennie and I displayed artfully in their windows. The working relationship led to friendship – reaffirmed every time we went, not only by the monetary reward, but, importantly, by a few slices of still-warm, gooey chocolate cake.

To reach Platanos, you turn off the Skiathos ring road, next to the bakery and pottery complex. The dust road rises, snaking up the mountainside, until it joins the monastery road at a T-junction. From there, you turn left and hardly 50 metres further, arrive at the Platanos taverna. It is a modern structure, entered at road level, through the garden, welcomed by purring cats sunning themselves, past the herb patches, and onto the topmost floor. The owner's home is downstairs. From the terrace, the view across the town of Skiathos to the islands beyond is breathtaking. As a family restaurant, it is accessed through the kitchen and family rooms! After a warm welcome, you are shown to a table. Father is a fisherman while the mother and two sons run the tavern. Over time and a developing friendship, we discovered the best dishes on the menu. A favourite of mine was Mamma's orange cake, a semolina and orange confection saturated with orange syrup, which we enjoyed ever so often. But no amount of flattery or hinting could secure the recipe. Mamma just smiled sweetly.

On one occasion I took a bottle of my plum jam as a gift to her. I was very proud of that particular batch: translucent ruby in colour, slightly jellied, a little tart and really plummy. Mamma received it with a modicum of appreciation, explaining that she would taste it and ask me for the recipe if she liked it. She didn't ever ask!

Blitz cake. Where does this name originate? I grew up with this cake, always thinking that Mom was quickly going to make a *blitskoek* (blitz cake). But it is not a quick recipe to bake. At one stage it occurred to me that it might have been a cake popular during the period of the London blitz. But that really sounds too far-fetched.

No matter about the name, we kept baking it – even changing the name superciliously while working at La Residence. I offered our guests an Apricot and Almond Macaroon Cake for afternoon tea. How pretentious and silly of me! Everyone really loved the combination of buttery cake, brittle meringue, slightly tart, poached fresh apricots and the nuttiness of the almonds.

A delicious alternative is to make a coconut macaroon topping, which, in turn, begs a filling of exotic fruit such as mango and/or granadilla. The cake may be served with a sorbet, crème fraîche (my personal favourite) or clotted cream.

$\mathcal{M}$ILLY NOIK'S
southern Georgia chocolate cake

750 ml cake flour
750 ml sugar
250 ml cocoa powder
15 ml baking powder
3 ml salt
250 g butter
15 ml vanilla essence
375 ml milk
3 eggs
60 ml fresh cream
icing sugar for dusting

Preheat the oven to 165 °C. Grease a 26-cm cake tin.

In a mixing bowl, sift together the flour, sugar, cocoa, baking powder and salt. In a saucepan, melt together the butter, vanilla essence and milk. Make a well in the centre of the dry ingredients, then pour in the melted mixture and mix thoroughly.

Add the eggs, one at a time, mixing them in very well. Lastly, pour in the cream and mix. Pour into the cake tin. Bake for 1 hour.

Leave to cool in the tin before turning out. Dust with icing sugar.

LITZ CAKE

whipped cream or apricot (or other fruit)
compote as filling
icing sugar for dusting

BATTER
110 g butter
80 ml castor sugar
4 large egg yolks (reserve the whites for
the meringue)
110 g cake flour sifted with 5 ml baking
powder
30 ml milk

MERINGUE
4 large egg whites
150 ml castor sugar
30 g blanched flaked almonds
10 ml white sugar mixed with 3 ml
ground cinnamon

Preheat the oven to 180 °C. Line 2 x 23-cm cake tins with baking paper.

Cream the butter and sugar. Add the egg yolks, one by one, then mix in just a little of the flour. Add the milk and whisk through. Fold in the rest of the flour mixture.

Divide the batter between the tins. Do not despair if it looks too mean.

For the meringue, whip the egg whites until stiff, but not dry. Add the castor sugar while whipping until it forms a smooth meringue. Divide between the tins and spread evenly over the batter. Sprinkle the almonds, and sugar-cinnamon over the two cakes. Bake for 30 minutes. Leave to cool slightly before turning them out.

To assemble, carefully place one cake, meringue side up, on a cake plate or stand. Spread with whipped cream, apricot or other fruit compote and place the second cake on top. The meringue makes these cakes very fragile, but a little crack or dent adds to their appeal. Dust generously with icing sugar.

Blits Koek:

1st Part:
4 egg yolks
1/4 lb. butter
1/2 cup sugar
1 cup flour
2 teaspoon B.P.
1/4 cup milk

2nd Part:
Beat whites of eggs
Add 3/4 cup sugar &
1 cup coconut.

Method: Cream butter & sugar, add egg yolks. Then milk & flour alternately & then B.P. Put in layer tins. Put mixture of 2nd part on top. Bake in slow oven. Spread jam between layers.

Moroccan pastures on the road between Fez and Rabat.

Crown the King
with Carrot-tops,
Dress him
in Sateen

Carrots, turnips, parsnips, kohlrabi, beetroot and radishes are underground treasures that ideally, should be sown *in situ*. As a child I loved watching the rows of seedlings grow, in slightly higgledy-piggledy lines, greener and greener. Then came a moment when the rows required thinning out. I loved helping my dad, carefully pulling out the extraneous ones to make space for the rest. Admittedly, I had pangs of guilt taking out the little ones, but the odd one was big enough to wash and eat. And that is how I learnt to eat vegetables. Other children's dislike of vegetables made no sense to me. And some children never grow up; a man recently refused Lennie's carrot cake, protesting that he does not eat vegetables and that the 'cake' was just a way of forcing him to eat carrots!

I do plead guilty to tempting our guests at La Residence in Franschhoek with servings of 'seasonal vegetables'. Carrots and turnips were often presented buttered and sprinkled with black onion seeds. Parsnips were oven baked and used as garnish, with the crispy tips adding sculpture to an ordinary dish. Kohlrabi was mashed with butter and nutmeg. These vegetables were frequently foreign to our guests, the Americans more so than the Europeans. Universal, though, was the enjoyment and testimony that 'I usually to not like vegetables, but these are delicious!'

Before the age of cholesterol, my older sister frequently made a dish of sweet potatoes, parsnips, tons of butter and treacle sugar. Baked in a medium oven for a long while, everything turned into a caramel delight. A mixture of carrots and parsnips was often similarly caramelised in a saucepan.

In Morocco we enjoyed the most tantalising mounds of couscous, tightly and decoratively packed with root vegetables: big carrots quartered lengthways, wedges of turnips and kohlrabi. There were also courgettes and long pieces of brinjal. All were usually boiled in flavourful stock and made to glisten with olive oil. They serve as a base for tagines, stewed meats in unctuous sauces or a simple tomato sauce, always complemented with *harissa* (hot chilli paste), *za'atar* (spice mix), chilli or *sumac* (berry seasoning).

The North Africans also know how to make the most delectable root vegetable pickles. Displayed in large jars at all eateries, they are spectacular. Lovely shapes and colours –

carrots, turnips, beetroot, peppers, onions and even cauliflower, celery and whole radishes. The vinegar for the paler vegetables is often tinted with beetroot colouring. A word of warning: I enjoyed delicious pickled, long peppers at a restaurant and opted for more of the same with my next meal. Strangely, my mouth caught fire at the first bite and I started weeping involuntarily. The sweet peppers and chillies all looked exactly the same!

Everybody invariably talks about the markets in Fez, in Marrakech, in the Atlas Mountains. But we saw the vegetable gardens of Morocco. Driving south along the Atlantic coast from Casablanca to Essaouira, the road was flanked by field upon field of vegetable gardens. From time to time there were huge trucks parked in lay-bys, a dozen or more people loading them with newly harvested vegetables. We were puzzled by the odd stick stuck upright in the soil alongside the road. Speared at the top was a courgette, carrot or beetroot. We were informed that they indicated the fields that were ready for harvesting. A prospective buyer would inspect the fields, buy the whole stretch and bring in his harvesters, lorries and loaders. Then off they would go to hawk the vegetables in their distant villages.

For miles and miles my recurring thought was: 'Please God, may this be organic.'

ARROT AND FETA
upside-down tart

750 g carrots, peeled
5 ml castor sugar
5 ml coriander seeds, toasted and crushed
a few sprigs of fresh thyme
30 ml butter
400 ml vegetable stock
salt and pepper to taste
some black olives, pitted
400 g feta cheese, cut into slabs
400 g puff pastry
thick yoghurt to serve

Cut the carrots into bâtons and place them in a saucepan. Add the sugar, crushed coriander seeds, 3–4 sprigs of thyme, butter and stock. If the liquid does not cover the carrots entirely, add some water, then bring to the boil and cook until tender. Remove the carrots from the liquid and reduce the sauce until it resembles a thick syrup. Season with salt and pepper, but bear in mind that the feta is salty.

Preheat the oven to 200 °C and line a rectangular baking dish or tin with non-stick baking paper.

Arrange the carrots crossways at the bottom of the dish, then scatter the olives over them. Place the slabs of feta on top and sprinkle with the carrot syrup. Finally, roll out the pastry to cover all, with a little extra to tuck in all the way around. Bake for 30 minutes until golden brown.

Leave the tart to cool for a while before running a knife around the outside and turning it out onto a platter. Serve garnished with a dollop of thick yoghurt and some sprigs of thyme or fresh salad leaves. The recipe could also be made into individual small tartlets. Serves 6 as a starter

BEEF
with root vegetables

30 ml olive oil
1 onion, sliced
2 small sprigs of fresh rosemary
4 sprigs of fresh thyme
3 fresh bay leaves
rind of 1 orange
250 ml dry red wine
1.5 kg topside or silverside, cut into generous cubes (±3 cm)
1 kg of various root vegetables (carrots, potatoes, turnips, kohlrabi, parsnips),
    cut into chunks
1 x 400 g can chopped tomatoes
salt and freshly ground black pepper

Make up a marinade by combining 1 tablespoon (15 ml) of the olive oil, the onion, rosemary, thyme, bay leaves, orange rind and red wine. Marinate the cubes of meat, covered, in the wine mixture, in a cool place for a few hours or overnight.

Preheat the oven to 180 °C.

Drain the meat (but reserve the marinade) and heat the remaining oil in a saucepan. Brown the meat in small batches and set aside. Scoop some onion from the marinade and brown this as well.

Place the meat and the root vegetables together in a heavy casserole dish. Pour the reserved marinade and the tomatoes over the meat. Season with the salt and pepper. Cover and place in the oven. After 20 minutes, reduce the heat to 160 °C and cook for 2 hours. Check from time to time to see that the liquid does not cook away. Add some water along the way if necessary. Should there be too much liquid, uncover the dish and allow the liquid to reduce in the oven.

Serve with a crusty French bread. Serves 6 as a main course

CROWN THE KING WITH CARROT-TOPS, DRESS HIM IN SATEEN

Salt, Mustard, Vinegar, Pepper

It is fascinating that such a small quantity of these ingredients can make such a big difference to a dish … a pinch of salt, a teaspoon of mustard, two tablespoons of vinegar, a sprinkling of pepper. Nor should one dismiss the endless variety and quality of salt or vinegar available, for instance, which can also influence a dish for the better (or worse).

The old-fashioned cruet set that was so part of the 'English table' is hardly seen nowadays. They could be quite elaborate, to convey salt and pepper, vinegar, oil and mustard, allowing the diner to flavour his food according to his taste.

This raises the contentious point of sensitive chefs being annoyed that diners should interfere with their perfectly flavoured foods. Celebrity cook and food writer Elizabeth David said '… to claim that any cook, however masterly and subtle his touch, can season all dishes to suit every palate seems to me to attribute to him the powers of a magician …!' This brings to mind my earliest efforts at seasoning my boiled egg all by myself!

⁂

Childhood memories of mustard revolved around the nastiness of sharp mustard: 'Never eat a grown-up ham sandwich – the mustard will take your breath away!' and 'Do not swear or say bad things, Mom will put mustard on your tongue!' Severely unattractive, but certainly effective, was the use of mustard as a poultice to rid a sore of poison.

We were still very young and anti-mustard when my aunt Hannetjie (Nanna to us) started making a sweet mustard sauce. Witnessing the can of sweet condensed milk going into the mixture sparked our interest, however, and very soon Nanna's sweet mustard sauce outdid any commercial tomato sauce in popularity at our table. Hardly a plate of food was not drowned in this sauce. The recipe was duly passed on and to this day I still enjoy this sauce which, in view of today's health consciousness, should long have disappeared from my diet. I suppose I use it in a different context these days: as a dipping sauce for crudités, as a sauce on the side of pink, seared fillet of beef or as a sauce for tiny steamed onions.

⁂

Vinegar pudding – of all the dumb things – is an absolute favourite in our family. I love making a fuss of serving it to our foreign friends, who invariably are perplexed, no doubt expecting a vinegar-sour confection … and then they ask for the recipe. Mine comes from Tant Martie, Philip du Toit's mom in De Aar. She was a wonderful cook who advocated the abundant use of butter and fat because 'it makes the food go down so easily!' Two days on the farm and one would succumb to numerous doses of *Lewensessens* (Essence of Life), a vile-tasting antidote to biliousness. Bless her! She could nurse you back to health in a thrice, ready for the next huge meal.

White pepper, black pepper, green pepper and pink pepper … how confusing. Yet, each has its own aromatic fragrance. White pepper has a sharpness and an almost scented aroma. The black peppercorn embodies the central white core as well as the outer husk. As it is ground, a special aroma is released that makes freshly ground black pepper much more desirable than the ready-ground variety, which loses its fragrance with time.

Green peppercorns from Madagascar used to be *de rigueur* with pepper steaks served in the 1970s.

In an interesting twist, both black and pink peppercorns are currently used in sweet dishes. A grinding of black pepper over strawberries or the beautiful pink dots of pink peppercorns with their sweet fragrance scattered around a berry panna cotta are both delicious combinations.

SAME-DAY BREAD AND BUTTER PICKLES

24 small cucumbers, thinly sliced
750 g onions, thinly sliced
90 ml salt
500 ml vinegar
500 g sugar
3 ml ground turmeric
60 ml white mustard seeds
10 ml celery seeds
2 ml cayenne pepper

Sterilise 3 x 500 ml honey jars.

Mix together the cucumbers, onions and salt. (The sharp and bitter juices will be extracted.) Leave to stand for a few hours, then rinse well and drain.

Combine the vinegar, sugar, turmeric, mustard seeds, celery seeds and cayenne pepper in a large saucepan and bring to the boil. Add the cucumbers and onions and bring it just to the boil again. Simmer for 2 minutes. (Do not really boil or you will lose the crispness of the cucumbers and onions.) While hot, pour into the prepared jars.

This pickle mixture does not need to stand for any length of time before using, hence its 'same day' name. It's delicious served with flatbread.

SALT, MUSTARD, VINEGAR, PEPPER

PICKLED LEMONS

**lemons with a thick, smooth skin, well
  washed
coarse salt**

Cut the lemons into quarters lengthways
(from the tail end towards the stem), but do
not cut all the way through.

Use plenty of coarse salt to fill the
quartered lemons. Pour some salt into the
bottom of a sterilised jar large enough to hold
a number of lemons. Place the first lemon on
the salt and pack subsequent lemons tightly
alongside and on top of this one. Pour more
salt onto the lemons.

Squeeze enough lemon juice to fill the jar
to the top and to cover the lemons completely.
Seal the jar.

Store in a cool dry place. Allow about
three months for the lemons to cure properly
before using. When you want to use the
lemons, discard the flesh and rinse the skin
under water. Serve in little dice or slivers
with salads or meat dishes to impart a most
exotic flavour.

VINEGAR PUDDING

BATTER

1 egg

125 ml sugar

250 ml cake flour, sifted

5 ml baking powder

5 ml bicarbonate of soda

a pinch of salt

25 ml apricot jam

25 ml vinegar

SYRUP

125 g butter

250 ml boiling water

250 ml milk

250 ml sugar

5 ml vanilla essence

125 ml brandy

Preheat the oven to 180 °C. Grease a 24 x 18-cm oven dish.

Beat the egg and sugar together until pale and light. Add the flour, baking powder, bicarbonate of soda and salt and fold them in. Stir in the apricot jam.

Prepare the syrup by placing all the syrup ingredients in a saucepan and heat until the butter has melted and the sugar dissolved. Boil for about 1 minute. Pour the syrup into the prepared oven dish.

Stir the vinegar into the batter then pour it slowly into the middle of the dish with the syrup, to form an island. Bake for 30 minutes. Serve hot with cream and/or custard. Serves 6

In the Mediterranean, sheep, goats
and olive groves are synonymous.

A Pitsilia region/Agros B C

Palodeia

1 KALAMIES

KOUNTOUROS

PAMPO

2 LOURIA

Troodos

Polemidia Dam.
10
KOKKINOGIA Panagia
Chrysafiliotissa
3 VIKLIA

Pano Polemidia PALIOMANTRES

13
Hospital Agia Anastasia 13

4

Panagia
Evangelistria 28

Kato Polemidia
Pafos A1

5

Pafos KOPRITSA

11
12

6 Industrial
Area

Maria had a Little Lamb

It was on a beautiful, clear Sunday morning that we drove west towards Pafos. After morning tea in Pafos we headed for Akamas, turned west at the coast and reached the Baths of Aphrodite, a green, watery spot overrun by tourists and ferns. Aphrodite must have been very clean as we visited her 'baths' in various Mediterranean spots!

On our way back we saw a sign pointing towards a seaside taverna, 'Takis' Taverna', and we realised this was Takis the Refugee! In Fig Tree Bay, ever searching for good postcards, we came upon a superb collection. One of the cards featured a handsome man at a table in his taverna. A beautiful composition, lots of blue and white and a taverna so typical that we longed to sit there with him. The legend on the back named him 'Takis the Refugee' (from the Turkish invasion in the north), who ran his taverna in Akamas.

We retraced our steps and turned into the dust road leading to the seaside. At the end of the track was the taverna. As we parked, we saw a man at a clay oven behind the building. He was breaking the clay seal, opening the oven from whence came the most appetising fragrance. We were witnessing the traditional way of preparing *kleftiko* (stolen lamb).

After introducing ourselves he asked where we were from.

'South Africa! I used to work in Port Elizabeth for my uncle!' Within minutes we learnt that he was a Greek Adonis in Port Elizabeth, that he thought South African girls beautiful and that his uncle was a slave driver. Takis also said that he made the best *kleftiko* in all of Cyprus. Turning to the oven, he poked a long fork into the cavity, wiggled it and brought out a most delectable piece of crispy lamb. Everything happened so spontaneously: I wanted the tit-bit so badly, Lennie is a no-red-meat person. Takis fed it into Lennie's gaping mouth, which was trying to say no-thank-you! Gracefully he said how good it was, explaining that he actually did not eat any red meat.

'What? Are you ill … what do you eat then?'

'Chicken,' Lennie said meekly.

'No bloody chicken in my taverna! Come, you look the feesh.'

It was amusing to see which portions and parts of the lamb were sent to the various tables. Takis wanted to know with each order who it was for. The Europeans got smaller portions with less fat. The English were served medium portions with reasonable amounts of crispy, fatty bits. The Greek Cypriots were served kilos of fatty, cholesterol-rich lamb.

But our new friend looked after us very well. Lennie's fish was fresh and grilled to perfection. My kilo of *kleftiko* was a Cypriot plate-full. He told us that it was *lamb*, not mutton, from his own farm. It was placed on a bed of herby branches inside the oven to benefit from the flavours and to allow the fat to drip onto the oven floor. It was the most delicious lamb of my life.

Greek Easter celebrations

MARIA HAD A LITTLE LAMB

THE EASTER LAMB

A word that causes confusion when transcribed from Greek into English, is 'lamb'. Greek is a highly phonetic language; all letters and syllables are pronounced. Having a 'b' at the end of a word and then ignoring it in pronunciation defies comprehension to Greeks. There also is no single letter with a 'b' sound in Greek. What we would see as 'ß' is in fact a 'v'. Two letters 'MΠ' combined, produces a b-sound. Thus menus in Greece frequently offer 'lamp'!

The Easter lamb is a non-negotiable tradition at this holiest of times. Every household must grill a lamb or join a family who is doing so. In 2001 Yalis and Katherine, our neighbours at Villa Athena on Skiathos, invited us to celebrate Easter with them. It was a blue-sky day and the lamb was on the spit. As the aroma spread, we became hungrier and hungrier. In true Greek-South African manner, Katherine, who hails from Mossel Bay, also had a spread for non lamb-eaters – much to Lennie's relief! I had to agree with him though, that to see a whole lamb – head and all – grilling on a spit, was daunting.

Our *Pasxa* (Easter) experience in Almyros, a small village south of Volos, was also very special. When we mentioned that we might spend Easter in Greece, our friend Yannis was adamant: we had to stay with the family in Almyros, his father's home village. We were fêted in every way possible, but Yannis drew the line when two of his uncles wanted us to 'make the Volta' (evening stroll) with them. In the morning, everyone strolled through the town, greeting friends with '*Xristos Agnesti*' (Christ has risen). We might have found the 'introduction of the foreigners to all and sundry' too much, he surmised!

Luncheon was the food event of the year. Two lambs were roasted simultaneously as there were many people, and each family insisted on having its own. The tables were laid with bright plastic cloths and colourful picnicware. With the wonderful food set out, it provided a festive atmosphere and an ambience that spoke of genuine hospitality, kindness and friendship. While the lambs were turning on the spits, we tried various *mezzethes*, this one's favourite dish, that one's secret recipe, a treat sent from Metsovo …

The music was playing with feet a-tapping. A few drops of ouzo, beer or wine later and some of the men were on their feet, making a few tentative moves. But as the music became more compelling, the dancing became more real. Dust billowed, hands clapped and fingers clicked. By the time the lamb was ready, everyone, now covered in dust and red-faced, was ravenous.

As silence settled over the tables, everyone was content with a lovely plate of food. From time to time there was a request for more *tzatziki*, salt, wine, salad … the Feast of the Lamb. After lunch, a little nap became imperative. However, before sunset, we strolled across the classical Plains of Thessaly in the golden aura of the setting sun.

Eggs dyed red, a Greek Easter tradition (top), the men take to their feet (centre), and (bottom) the Plains of Thessaly at sunset.

YOUVETSI ME ARNAKI
(Rice noodles with lamb)

Rice noodles, orzo, kritharaki, *pasta rice … all the same thing. It is quite confusing as the appearance is that of rice, but the texture and taste is that of pasta. These little things are, in fact, pasta. Whenever I see them around, I buy some as they are not a regular commodity on the pasta shelves in South Africa.*

'Youvetsi' refers to a baked dish of orzo in which one can have buried lamb, chicken, seafood or vegetables. In restaurants they usually serve this meal in individual pottery dishes. As family fare, youvetsi *can also be made using a whole shoulder or a few shins of lamb. The bones and fatty bits protruding, brown and sizzling, make the dish mouthwateringly attractive. In a similar way one can bury chicken pieces, seafood or vegetables in orzo as well. My first ever taste of* youvetsi *was actually lamb and that is the recipe below.*

60 ml olive oil
1 kg lamb fillet (neck or shoulder is ideal), cubed
1 large onion, roughly chopped
1 x 400 g can chopped tomatoes
5 ml sugar or honey
salt and freshly ground black pepper to taste
375 ml orzo
100 g Kefalotiri cheese or a flavoursome pecorino or Parmesan
fresh basil leaves to garnish

Preheat the oven to 180 °C.

Heat the oil in a saucepan and fry the meat, sealing it and browning on all sides. Fry it in small batches at a time to ensure that the meat is fried, not stewed. Remove from the saucepan and set aside.

Brown the onion in the same saucepan, then return the meat to the pan. Add the tomatoes, sugar or honey, and salt and pepper. Cook until the meat it is very tender – usually about 45 minutes, so it may be necessary to add some water. Stir from time to time to avoid catching. Remove from the heat and stir in the orzo. Transfer to a deep oven dish. The mixture should only fill the dish halfway to allow for the expansion of the pasta. Fill the dish with hot water (or I sometimes have some vegetable stock on hand) to just cover the orzo. Stir gently.

Bake for 30–40 minutes. All the liquid should be absorbed, but the dish must not be dry. Sprinkle with the cheese and return to the oven to brown.

This dish is best served piping hot. Garnish with basil leaves. In Greece this dish is served on its own, but you could serve it with a green salad. Serves 6 as a main course

ARIRA

*There are many versions of this Moroccan soup (*harira *is the word for soup in Morocco), but I enjoy the simplicity and flavour of this one. If you include some lamb soup bones, it will enhance the taste of the soup.*

30 ml olive oil
1 large onion, finely chopped
2 cloves garlic, crushed and chopped
500 g lamb shoulder or leg, trimmed and cut into pieces
a few lamb soup bones (optional)
10 ml ground cumin
5 ml ground coriander
10 ml sweet paprika
15 ml grated fresh ginger
1 litre water
2 x 400 g cans chickpeas
2 x 400 g cans chopped tomatoes
45 ml tomato paste
1 small bunch fresh parsley, chopped
1 small bunch fresh coriander, chopped
black olives to serve
harissa to taste
fresh flat-leaf parsley to garnish

Heat the oil in a saucepan and cook the onion until translucent and golden. Add the garlic and cook for a few seconds. Remove all from the saucepan and set aside.

In the same saucepan, brown the meat (and bones if using) in batches. Add the spices to the meat and cook for approximately 1 minute to release the fragrance. Return the onion and garlic to the pot. Pour in the water and bring to the boil.

Add the chickpeas, chopped tomatoes and tomato paste and allow the soup to simmer for at least 1 hour. Stir from time to time. The meat must be very, very tender. Add some more water if it reduces too much, but do aim for a creamy consistency. Sprinkle the parsley and coriander into the soup and boil for another 15 minutes. Remove the bones.

Serve with a scattering of black olives, and/or a scoop of harissa. Garnish with parsley. Serves 6 as a starter

GREEK LAMB AND POTATOES
with lemon and origanum

2–3 cloves garlic
3 kg lamb (leg or shoulder)
125 ml lemon juice
30 ml dried origanum
salt and freshly ground black pepper
1 large onion, sliced
1 kg potatoes, peeled and cut into large wedges

Preheat the oven to 180 °C.

Slice the garlic into slivers and, with a small, sharp knife, cut cavities into the meat and insert the garlic neatly. Moisten the meat all over with half of the lemon juice, then sprinkle with the origanum, salt and pepper. Place the meat into a baking dish, cover with aluminium foil and roast for about 1 hour.

If there is any fat in the dish, drain it at this point. Add the onion slices and a cup (250 ml) of water to the pan and baste the lamb with it. Roast, uncovered, in a cooler oven (160 °C) for another hour. Turn and baste occasionally, so that the meat has an even colour.

Arrange the potatoes around the lamb and baste them with the pan juices. Douse with the rest of the lemon juice and sprinkle with more origanum and season with salt and pepper. Bake for another hour, but check constantly to baste and add drops of water if necessary. Turn the potatoes from time to time.

To serve, cut the lamb into pieces rather than slicing it. Plate the meat and potatoes with a generous serving of the pan juices. Serves 6 as a main course

Four and Twenty Blackbirds

There were many more than 24 blackbirds …

In a large, attractive canister, rather like a cookie jar, nestled little round bundles, whitish in colour, in a clear liquid. Not for one moment, since we were in a taverna, did I equate them with little late birds in a pickling solution like formaldehyde.

Our Cypriot hosts were generous to a fault. We had become fond of certain dishes and they were duly ordered. Pavlos went straight to the kitchen and also organised more dishes. He also pointed to the cookie jar.

The table groaned. Bowls and dishes with more food were placed on top of water glasses to build a second storey. Then came a large oval platter of the little round bundles, nestling in bunches of the lushest mint I had ever seen.

'These,' Pavlos announced, 'are very special. You will not find them everywhere. Please, have one and take it with some mint leaves.' Lennie understood and his vegetarian instincts took over. I sat with an embryonic-looking dead bird on my plate, sad and nauseating. The only hope I had was the mint.

Worse was to come though, with Pavlos showing me how to eat the creature. Spear the little darling in the breast and gut it with a full sweep of the knife. That meant that the innards were still there! It was surprisingly easy to clean the birdie and, smiling feebly, I wrapped it in a shroud of several mint leaves and tried to eat it in one go. However, due to the size of the bird I was forced to have a second mouthful. It was tender from the pickling potion, but not all the little bones and other hard things such as beak and feet had softened …

'Thanks,' I said, 'how extraordinary.'

'Have the last one, then!'

You do not go against a kind Cypriot host. You do not offend, even if you have completely lost your appetite.

Catching (or procuring) these little birds is no longer legal. They used to set up nets in which the flocks became entangled. Goodness knows how many perished annually in this manner. The birds were a species of swallow that flew in from other parts of the world, just like the tourists, but, unlike tourists who went home to their countries fat and tanned, these poor creatures stayed behind, in large glass jars. This was a recipe I did not request!

The Old Cataract Hotel in Aswan, Egypt (top and centre), and with our Swiss friend Reina and Mr Foui on his felucca (bottom).

184   FOUR AND TWENTY BLACKBIRDS

ℰGYPTIANS LOVE TO EAT PIGEON

Travelling to Alexandria, all along the delta, you see small and some large towns, each with its pigeon towers. These are fascinating mud structures like oversized beehives, patterned with nesting holes, brickwork courses, sticks protruding in all directions, resting places for the pigeons. Everywhere there were swarms of pigeons.

In the gardens of the Winter Palace Hotel in Luxor, there was a lovely pigeon tower – not unlike a large ethnic sculpture. It was there, in Luxor, that our taxi driver dropped us off at a restaurant purported to provide good Egyptian fare. The menu offered pigeon and I was tempted – especially as a dish of pigeon was carried past our table to an Egyptian madame sitting all by herself. She was one of those fascinating women with a fair complexion, wearing a little too much make-up, somewhat overdressed and, judging by her jewellery, affluent. She wasted no time in attacking her dinner. It was an astounding display of dexterity – fingers, mouth, teeth and tongue. In went a little wing. Munch, munch. Out came a bundle of bones, propelled from tongue to floor. I decided against ordering the pigeon and we turned our chairs just slightly in the other direction. Even the chicken dish on the menu was not an attractive option anymore. We probably had Nile perch or vegetables instead.

At sunset we went down the steps, through the garden of the Old Cataract Hotel in Aswan, to a little jetty on the Nile. Mr Foni was waiting for us in his *felucca*. He welcomed us on board his spotlessly clean and newly painted boat and soon we were drifting down the Nile, seeing Aswan from a different angle. Past the Elephantine Island, the Aga Khan's mausoleum, past peasant houses. Mr Foni rinsed some tea glasses in the Nile water and offered us some hibiscus tea. We were hesitant at first. Our one consolation was that we had seen the water being boiled! Cruising slowly, we watched as the sun set, reclining and relaxing and sipping the delicious tea.

From nowhere, a tiny craft propelled by two pairs of hands clutching homemade plywood offcut paddles, bore down on us. Two young urchins were singing at the top of their voices: 'Sur la Ponte d'Avignon, on y danse, on y danse …' Not quite what one would call relaxing sunset entertainment, but they meant well. A few *baksheesh* (small denomination notes) did not do the trick and they repeated their song, but thankfully another passing *felucca* was enough reason to lure them away. As the makeshift boat turned away from us we saw the misspelt name on the prow: *Peigon*.

'Baksheesh please!' (top and centre), a pigeon tower (bottom left), and feluccas on the Nile, Aswan (bottom right).

QUAILS
stuffed with leeks, apple and celery

The closest I ever came to blackbirds or pigeons was when I discovered the deboned quails supplied by Sue Baker of Wild Peacock in Stellenbosch. These are farmed birds of excellent quality.

olive oil
2 leeks, chopped
2 sticks celery, sliced
2 Granny Smith apples, peeled and diced
salt and freshly ground black pepper to taste
4 deboned quails
250 ml dry red wine
60 ml dark soy sauce
30 ml balsamic vinegar
fresh watercress or rocket leaves to garnish

Preheat the oven to 180 °C.

Pour a little olive oil into a frying pan and braise the leeks and celery until they are quite tender. Mix in the apples and season with the salt and pepper.

Stuff the birds with this mixture and secure the openings with a toothpick or two. Arrange them in a baking dish. Pour the red wine over them and cover the dish with a lid or aluminium foil. Bake for 45 minutes.

Remove from the oven, then pour the pan juices into a saucepan. Add the soy sauce and balsamic vinegar. Reduce this to treacly 'syrup' over a medium heat.

Return the quails to the oven and roast until brown. A little drizzle of olive oil or a knob of butter on the breast helps the browning process.

Serve on a bed of soft polenta napped with the syrupy reduction. Garnish with watercress or rocket. Serves 4 as a main course

AVGOLEMONO CHICKEN SOUP

*Avgo are eggs and lemono are lemons in Greek. Add some good stock …
how I love this combination!*

1 onion
1 carrot, thickly sliced
1–2 fresh or dried bay leaves
1 whole chicken
1.5 litres water
salt and freshly ground black pepper
125 ml uncooked rice
3 eggs, separated
45 ml lemon juice
1 litre hot chicken stock
a small bunch fresh Italian flat-leaf parsley

Place the onion, carrot, bay leaves and chicken in a saucepan and add the water. Season with the salt and pepper and bring to the boil. Simmer until the chicken is really tender.

Remove the chicken and leave it to cool. Strain the stock into another saucepan (discard the vegetables), then add the rice. Boil until the rice is tender.

Cut the chicken into pieces, remove the bones, skin and all other bits, retaining only the solid pieces of meat. Whisk the egg whites until stiff peaks form. Beat the yolks lightly then fold into the egg whites. Gently beat in the lemon juice. Combining this mixture with the hot stock can be tricky. Keep the stock hot, but do not boil. Start by slowly adding only about half a cup (125 ml) of stock to the egg mixture, beating all the time. Repeat this once more. Add the warmed egg mixture to the rest of the hot stock while whisking. Now add the chicken pieces.

The soup must remain velvety. It will curdle if it boils. Taste and adjust seasoning if necessary. Serve with a generous sprinkling of parsley. Serves ±6 as a starter

Recipe index

CONVERSION CHART

METRIC	US CUPS	IMPERIAL
1 ml	¼ tsp	–
2–3 ml	½ tsp	–
4 ml	¾ tsp	–
5 ml	1 tsp	³⁄₁₆ fl oz
15 ml	1 Tbsp	½ fl oz
25 ml	–	1 fl oz
50 ml	–	2 fl oz
60 ml	4 Tbsp	2 fl oz
80 ml	⅓ cup	2¾ fl oz
125 ml	½ cup	4 fl oz
200 ml	¾ cup	7 fl oz
250 ml	1 cup	9 fl oz
25 g	–	1 oz
50 g	–	2 oz
75 g	–	3 oz
100 g	–	4 oz
150 g	–	5 oz
200 g	–	7 oz
250 g	–	9 oz
500 g	–	1 lb 2 oz
750 g	–	1 lb 10 oz
1 kg	–	2 lb 4 oz

OVEN TEMPERATURES

°C CELSIUS	°F FAHRENHEIT	GAS MARK
100 °C	200 °F	¼
110 °C	225 °F	¼
120 °C	250 °F	1
140 °C	275 °F	1
150 °C	300 °F	2
160 °C	325 °F	3
180 °C	350 °F	4
190 °C	375 °F	5
200 °C	400 °F	6
220 °C	425 °F	7
230 °C	450 °F	8
240 °C	475 °F	9